TOO FEW TOMORROWS

Appalachian Consortium Press
Boone, North Carolina 28608

TOO FEW TOMORROWS

Urban Appalachians In the 1980's

*Edited by Phillip J. Obermiller &
William W. Philliber*

Library of Congress Cataloging-in-Publication Data

Too Few Tomorrows.
Bibliography: p.
Includes index.
1. Ethnicity- Appalachian Region, Southern.
2. Ethnology- Appalachian Region, Southern. 3. Regionalism-
Appalachian Region, Southern. 4. Appalachian Region, Southern-
Social conditions. 5. Appalachian Region, Southern- Social life and
customs.
I. Obermiller, Phillip J. II. Philliber, William W., 1943-
F217.A65T66 1986 975 86-28816
ISBN 0-913239-47-X (pbk.)

THE APPALACHIAN CONSORTIUM

The Appalachian Consortium is a non-profit educational organization comprised of institutions and agencies located in the Southern Highlands. Our members are volunteers who plan and execute projects which serve 156 mountain counties in seven states. Among our goals are:

Preserving the cultural heritage of Southern Appalachia
Protecting the mountain environment
Improving the educational opportunities for area students and teachers
Conducting scientific, social and economic research
Promoting a positive image of Appalachia
Encouraging regional cooperation

THE MEMBER INSTITUTIONS OF THE APPALACHIAN CONSORTIUM ARE:

Appalachian State University

Blue Ridge Parkway

East Tennessee State University

Great Smoky Mountains Natural History Association

John C. Campbell Folk School

Lees-McRae College

Mars Hill College

Mountain Regional Library

North Carolina Division of Archives and History

Southern Highlands Handicraft Guild

U.S. Forest Service

Warren Wilson College

Western Carolina University

Western North Carolina Historical Society

TABLE OF CONTENTS

PREFACE, *Maureen R. Sullivan* — i

PART I: FROM SOCIAL PROBLEM TO ETHNIC GROUP — 1

1. TOO FEW TOMORROWS, *Thomas E. Wagner* — 3

2. A DECADE IN REVIEW: The Development of the Ethnic Model in Urban Appalachian Studies, *Michael E. Maloney* — 13

3. APPALACHIANS IN MIDWESTERN CITIES: Regionalism as a Basis of Ethnic Group Formation, *William W. Philliber and Phillip J. Obermiller* — 19

4. URBAN APPALACHIANS & CANADIAN MARITIME MIGRANTS: Comparative Study of Emergent Ethnicity, *Martin N. Marger and Phillip J. Obermiller* — 23

5. LABELING URBAN APPALACHIANS, *Phillip J. Obermiller* — 35

6. THE ETHNIC ENTREPRENEUR IN THE URBAN APPALACHIAN COMMUNITY, *Sharlotte K. Neely* — 43

PART II: CONTINUING DEVELOPMENT AMONG APPALACHIAN MIGRANTS — 49

7. MOVING ON: Recent Patterns of Appalachian Migration, *Phillip J. Obermiller and Robert W. Oldendick* — 51

8. THE CHANGING COMPOSITION OF APPALACHIAN MIGRANTS, *William W. Philliber* — 63

PART III: FROM REGIONALISM TO URBAN LIFE — 67

9. TWO STUDIES OF APPALACHIAN CIVIC INVOLVEMENT, *Phillip J. Obermiller and Robert W. Oldendick* — 69

10. THE IMPACT OF THE URBAN MILIEU ON THE APPALACHIAN FAMILY TYPE, *James K. Crissman.* — 81

11. EFFECTS OF SCHOOLS & SCHOOLING UPON APPALACHIAN CHILDREN IN CINCINNATI, *Michael E. Maloney and Kathryn M. Borman.* — 89

12. APPALACHIAN YOUTH IN CULTURAL TRANSITION, *Clyde B. McCoy and H. Virginia McCoy* — 99

13. BLACK APPALACHIAN MIGRANTS: The Issue of Dual Minority Status, *William W. Philliber and Phillip J. Obermiller* — 111

CONCLUSION: The Future for Appalachians in Urban Areas, *William W. Philliber* — 117

BIBLIOGRAPHY — 123

CONTRIBUTORS — 139

INDEX — 141

PREFACE

Maureen R. Sullivan

Between 1940 and 1970 an estimated three million people left their home places in Appalachia in search of jobs. Many migrated to industrial centers in the Midwest and settled in cities like Cincinnati, Chicago, and Detroit. Although they were, in a way, "just looking for a home"–a better life for themselves and their families–many did not find the promised land they sought. The fate of perhaps a third of the migrants was to become long-term dwellers in the underclass.

But even for those who made it into secure blue-collar employment, the dream was not without pain. Both research and personal experience point to a socially different group of people who are struggling with questions of identity, rootlessness, and cultural negation. Research done in Northern Kentucky indicates that a sizeable number of urban Appalachians there do not regard the area as home even if they were born or long settled in Northern Kentucky communities. For them, home is a family place in the hills of Eastern Kentucky.

Brenda Ann Nix, an Appalachian woman living in Northern Kentucky, writes poignantly about the experiences of her family:

> Mamau and Papau lived around Corbin and Pathfork, Kentucky. We never called ourselves Appalachians. Still we have things in common. I remember intense religious services. One of my uncles was a Holiness preacher who could touch snakes when he was in the Spirit. . .Mamau and Papau moved to Detroit but home remained Corbin and Pathfork. Mamau was leery of foreigners. Detroit was a strange city. . .You know my mom hates being called a hillbilly. She thinks it's a put down. I've known people who liked the country accent. Others looked at it as a sign of ignorance. And me–I'm still trying to understand me and my family. . . Papau worked in the coal mines. Mamau just kept trusting her Bible and all the while their children felt the strain.

i

As the third generation of mountain people, I feel sometimes ashamed of my background–sometimes I'm proud. Appalachians. . .I've never known a tougher people.

Her words address the dichotomy of being an "urban Appalachian" with its combination of pride and pain, with the constant question, "What does it mean to be who I am?"

This book addresses some of the contemporary questions facing urban Appalachians. It is, I believe, the third part of a trilogy which began with *The Invisible Minority: Urban Appalachians,* a book which focused on migration and documented the early experiences of Appalachian migrants. Next came *Appalachian Migrants in Urban America: Cultural Conflict or Ethnic Group Formation?* which compared first- and second-generation Appalachians with other groups in the city. This volume continues the tradition of documenting Appalachian migration and settlement patterns by presenting current information on urban Appalachian social movements and leadership, on new trends in migration, and on social problems faced by urban Appalachians.

The past decade has seen three issues dominate the study of Appalachians who have migrated to urban areas outside of the region. One of the most important of these is the context in which Appalachian migrants and their descendents are to be viewed. The most developed analogy indicates that in many ways Appalachians can best be understood as an ethnic group. Yet challenges remain suggesting that they can be better understood in the larger context of class relationships while some maintain that there is simply nothing to understand. Part I of this volume presents those developments which have led to the increasing belief that Appalachian migrants and their descendents have become an ethnic group in the urban areas where they moved. Continuing a long tradition in the study of Appalachians, the second issue documents the magnitude and characteristics of Appalachians moving from the region. This issue has become more critical in recent years as interest has focused on migration into the area to the neglect of those leaving. However, as Part II of this volume illustrates, people continue to move out of Appalachia into the urban areas of the Midwest. Part III presents findings from a lesser-developed side of research on urban Appalachians–their participation in the urban milieu. These papers document participation in politics, family, and education as well as analyzing what it is to be young and Black as an Appalachian outside of the region.

PART ONE

From Social Problem To Ethnic Group

The past decade has witnessed a change in the framework used to study and understand people who migrated from Appalachia to urban centers in the Midwest. Prior to the mid-seventies these migrants were usually seen as a social problem. Journalists and social scientists competed to see who could describe the most poignant examples of maladjustment. While the documentation of social problems was successful, serious observers began to question whether the identification of these people as Appalachians added anything to understanding their experiences. Their problems might develop because they were rural to urban migrants, because they were migrants from the South to the North, because they were of lower socioeconomic status, or just because they were migrants. It was not enough to document that people from Appalachia had problems; it was necessary to demonstrate that those problems could not be explained from other existing frameworks.

In the mid-seventies people of Appalachian descent living outside the region began to be viewed as an ethnic group. The shift from social problem to ethnic group was brought about by both academic and political forces. Ethnicity was a major topic among social scientists. Models of ethnic pluralism had arisen in contrast to the assimilation model which had dominated the field for a number of years. Appalachians were included among those groups for whom an ethnic analogy was made. Politically it was useful to treat Appalachians as an ethnic group. Those groups who were recognized as such were eligible for private and public funds as well as legislative protection from discrimination.

The chapters contained in this section describe the work of political organizers and social scientists in applying the ethnic analogy to people of Appalachian descent living outside the region. The Urban Appalachian Council, under the leadership of Michael Maloney, provided the political organization from which the ethnic analogy emerged. Under its auspices a group of researchers, merely asked to study Appalachians, began to make an ethnic analogy. This work went in two related directions. The first step was to determine to what extent Appalachians were an ethnic group. The second step was to try and understand the causes for such an ethnic group formation. These papers describe both the process and the results of that work.

1

TOO FEW TOMORROWS

Thomas E. Wagner

According to demographers the movement of rural people to urban industrial centers continued nearly unabated for thirty years following World War II. Traditional port-of-entry neighborhoods in urban areas, which in years past received migrants of urban ethnic origin, were receiving centers for white rural to urban migrants. In numerous midwestern industrial centers, the greatest influx of rural to urban migrants were from the Southern Appalachian region. Estimates are that as many as seven million people permanently migrated out of the Southern Appalachian region during the 1940's, 1950's, and 1960's. Called "the great migration," this movement may be one of the most significant migrations of this century (Brown and Hillery, 1962).

During the 1940's a booming war-stimulated economy attracted Appalachian migrants to Detroit, Chicago, Cincinnati, and other manufacturing cities where plenty of jobs were available for unskilled labor. The region's net population loss due to migration during the forties was 705,894 persons (Brown and Hillery, 1962:58). During the fifties, automation and the switch to natural gas as a primary fuel brought mass unemployment to the eastern Kentucky and West Virginia coal fields and 1,569,000 left the region looking for work elsewhere. During the 1960's, the push/pull of regional unemployment and the promise of work served to keep the migration stream flowing, even though at a slower rate. Between 1960 and 1970, 592,000 people migrated out of the mountains (Brown, 1971). This migration of Appalachians to midwestern cities is nearly as great as Irish and Italian immigration in the late 1800's, and is much larger than the recent migration of Asians to this country. It was a mass movement of people that has gone largely unnoticed, perhaps, in part, because the migrants were white rural people moving from one part of the United States to another.

With little variation, the reasons for migrating were nearly always the same: the desire to improve one's economic status, and the knowledge of a relative living in an urban location (Hyland, 1972; Harmeling, 1969). Throughout the stories told to Gitlin and Hollander by Chicago's uptown residents, there is the consistent theme of moving north then south and then north again, depending upon economic conditions and family circumstances: "They go to Ohio, go up here to Chicago, or to Michigan or to somewhere around there because there is no work whatsoever–any real good paying jobs–in Harlan" (Gitlin and Hollander, 1970:263).   Often migration in one direction or the other occurs immediately following a change in family status, a death, separation, divorce, or marriage (Gitlin and Hollander; 1970, Harmeling, 1969). Personnel officers in many northern manufacturing companies followed the common practice of filling vacancies by asking workers from the mountains to notify some of their relatives (Cincinnati Human Relations Committee, 1956). Schwarzweller, Brown, and Manglam (1971) verify the recruiting efficiency of such kinfolk messages. In some plants in Cincinnati, the number of Kentucky-born workers was reported to be as high as 50-70% of the work staff.

The migratory streams were generally regional in nature, with individuals from certain areas or counties tending to move to the same northern destination. Migrants from eastern Kentucky counties came to southwestern Ohio, while those from West Virginia "headed out" for northeastern Ohio. Thus, Cincinnati, Hamilton, and Dayton, Ohio are commonly known as "Kentucky cities," while Columbus, Cleveland, and Akron are known as "West Virginia cities" (Brown, 1971).

The Cincinnati metropolitan area, including the counties in north central Kentucky and southeastern Indiana, was one of the primary receiving centers for Appalachian migrants from eastern Kentucky and adjacent West Virginia counties. It is estimated that over 100,000 migrants moved to the Cincinnati area during the thirty years of the "great migration." When one adds the children born to these migrants, the first and second generation Cincinnati area urban Appalachian population is estimated at over 213,000 people (Obermiller and Oldendick, 1984).

In Cincinnati and other midwestern urban areas, Appalachian migrants did not find the same ethnic "melting pot" found by earlier immigrant groups. There was no migrant infrastructure, with its economic opportunities and support services of so much benefit to earlier immigrant groups, to improve the quality of urban life for Appalachians moving to the city. The plight of urban areas after World War II was one of shrinking revenues, continued urban sprawl, "white flight," and strained social services. The large influx of rural to urban migrants created additional pressures and problems for urban social welfare, educational, health, and justice systems. As a result, urban Appalachians, as they came to be called, were largely ignored and misunderstood by city residents and service agencies. In some instances, the neglect was made worse by prejudicial actions toward the "hillbillies," "ridge runners," and "briar hoppers."

In Cincinnati, the response to this neglect was the formation of a coalition of individuals from diverse backgrounds and with an uncommon commitment to bring about improvements in the quality of life of the city's urban Appalachians. The primary objective of this paper is to trace the development of the Appalachian avocacy organizations which emerged within the migrant community.

Although ad hoc groups came together in some other midwestern cities to work on behalf of migrant Appalachians, it is the Urban Appalachian Council of

Cincinnati, its forerunners and affiliate groups, that is synonymous with the "urban Appalachian movement." One can only be impressed by the gains and accomplishments of this organization on behalf of urban Appalachians particularly, in the Cincinnati metropolitan area.

The history of the urban Appalachian movement in Cincinnati goes back to the early 1950's. A fairly large group of individuals and agencies including the Mayor's Friendly Relations Committee–the predecessor of the Cincinnati Human Relations Commission–Berea College and the Council of Southern Mountains developed an interest in the problems caused by mountain-to-urban migration. Virginia Coffey, former Director of the Cincinnati Human Relations Commission described the early days as follows:

> The Cincinnati Urban Appalachian Council is a reality today because of the foresight, interest, and determination of a few individuals. Back in 1948-49 Marshall Bragdon, then Executive Director of the Mayor's Friendly Relations Committee and I, the Assistant Director, were the city's lone human relations professionals. In carrying out our job to ensure justice, racial and religious freedom and equality for all citizens of Cincinnati, it soon became apparent that adjustment problems facing Black migrants from the rural South were similarly common to Appalachian migrants from the hills of Virginia, Kentucky, and Tennessee. While making this city aware of discrimination and unequal treatment to its Black minority, we also felt compelled to call attention to the plight of urban Appalachian migrants. (*Mountain Life and Work, 1976:19*)

Marshall Bragdon, in addition to his duties as Director of the Mayor's Friendly Relations Commission, served on the Executive Committee of the Council of Southern Mountains, located in Berea, KY, where he developed a lasting friendship with Perley Ayer, the charismatic leader of the Council. Bragdon's intense interest in the migration of Appalachian people brought early solid linkages between the mountains and the city. Virginia Coffey, Assistant Director under Bragdon and later Director, organized many local efforts to aid migrants, and began to build a constituency of concern among a wide range of the city's citizens. The Mayor's Friendly Relations Committee's commitment went well beyond expressing verbal concern. They sponsored several workshops, the first in April, 1954, where the keynote speaker was Roscoe Giffin, a professor from Berea College. The workshop was based on several assumptions:

1. The heavy migration from the hills will continue;
2. The newcomers' urban adjustment is vital to the city;
3. Too many make a poor adjustment: agencies and institutions don't know how to help the migrants;
4. Active intercultural study of this problem would yield facts, insights, and techniques of practical value; and
5. De-stereotyping the city man's and urban agencies' views of, and attitudes towards hillfolks is a vital first step in affecting

migrants' view and behavior (Cincinnati Human Relations Commission, 1956).

It is interesting to note that these objectives are similar to the objectives of the Appalachian Committee, established in 1972 by Frank Foster, Louise Spiegel, Stuart Faber, Mike Maloney, and others with the support of the Cincinnati Human Relations Commission.

There was a great deal of activity in Cincinnati following the 1954 workshop. An Episcopalian "ministry to mountaineers" began in 1955 and the Emanuel Community Center developed services to "hill families" funded by a grant from the Appalachian Fund. The Emanuel Community Center program resulted from the efforts of Ray Drukker, the Executive Director of the Appalachian Fund, Inc. Drukker began efforts to develop a Cincinnati program after he read a series of articles about the problems encountered by Appalachian migrants in the *Cincinnati Enquirer*.

In 1959, a team of eleven Cincinnatians representing the public schools, social services, police, and churches participated with teams from seven other cities in a three-week workshop at Berea College sponsored by the Council of Southern Mountains and led by Perley Ayer. Each team member was required to develop materials and educational programs for city agencies and services in support of Appalachian migrants in greater Cincinnati. These activities seemed promising, and by 1960 Marshall Bragdon was able to write, "The future looks fruitful. Yes, much has happened since 1954" (Cincinnati Human Relations Commission, 1956:2).

During the 1960's, a small cadre of committed individuals continued to work diligently on behalf of Appalachians in Cincinnati. Among this group was Stuart Faber, a trustee of the Appalachian Fund, and President of the Council of Southern Mountains; Louise Spiegel, a volunteer at the Mayor's Friendly Relations Committee, who helped coordinate many conferences and to consolidate membership of the early organizations; Frank Foster, a former college president who had retired to Cincinnati; and Ernie Mynatt, an outreach social worker at Emanuel Community Center.

Under the leadership of Stuart Faber, the Appalachian Fund provided a grant to the Emanuel Community Center to hire a social worker to work in the Over-the-Rhine area as a "detached" social worker providing services to Appalachians. After limited success by two different workers, the Center hired Ernie Mynatt. The Council of the Southern Mountains formally commissioned Mynatt's work by presenting him a "certificate" signed by Perley Ayer. In 1964, the Cincinnati Archdiocese provided funding for the establishment of the Main Street Bible Center directed by Father John Porter and Sister Shirley Gallahan. Shortly thereafter, Mike Maloney, a young migrant mountaineer, started working at the HUB Social Services Center, a multi-service social welfare agency in the Over-the-Rhine.

The primary energy for the Bible Center effort came from dozens of young volunteers, mostly Roman Catholic seminarians and nuns or former nuns and seminarians. The Bible Center and Old St. Mary's Catholic Church in Over-the-Rhine became the base of operations for this small army of volunteers who did door-to-door home visiting and conducted recreation activities and Bible classes for children and teens. Some of the volunteers lived in tenement apartments in the manner of a previous generation of settlement house workers. With this corps of inner-city volunteers and the support of the Archdiocese and Virginia Coffey, who during this period was Director of Memorial Community Center, Ernie Mynatt was able to begin support services directly aimed at the Appalachian migrants and displaced Blacks from Cincinnati's West End urban renewal areas. Many of the Bible Center volunteers became community organizers, social workers, and teachers in the inner city and continued to work on behalf of Appalachian migrants in these roles.

"The Hub" (not an acronym originally) was opened in 1966 as a branch of Memorial Community Center. It was a storefront social service agency staffed by professional as well as indigenous workers including migrants from eastern Kentucky. In 1968, HUB Services was funded as one of fourteen Pilot Cities Centers, the predecessor program to Model Cities.

It was not long before a coalition formed between Mynatt, Maloney, and others working out of the Emanuel Center, HUB Services, and Main Street Bible Center. This loose coalition made its first attempt at organization in 1969 when Maloney and Mynatt formed the United Appalachians of Cincinnati (UAC). The organization was organized to "promote the self-awareness and self-activity of the Appalachian people in Cincinnati, to encourage our urban institutions, respond to the needs and interest of Appalachians, and to show the community-at-large the power and beauty of our culture" (Maloney, unpublished).

Membership in the United Appalachians of Cincinnati was accomplished by joining the Council of the Southern Mountains. By-laws were drawn up and about fifty individuals were listed as members of the organization. The group disbanded when Mike Maloney left Cincinnati to attend graduate school in North Carolina. However, Frank Foster, Louise Spiegel, and Stuart Faber kept the coalition together by calling periodic meetings of an "Appalachian Committee," an organization open to anyone who was willing to attend the meetings. The movement was at a crucial but formative stage and a number of individuals who would later provide important voluntary support for the Urban Appalachian Council were recruited into the movement.

In 1970 Ernie Mynatt received a grant from the Appalachian Fund and opened the Appalachian Identity Center. Its importance was that it was the first support and advocacy program anywhere in the midwest run by urban Appalachians themselves. Ernie Mynatt directed the Center while continuing his work as a detached social worker on the streets in Over-the-Rhine. The youth attending the Appalachian Identity Center formed the Sons and Daughters of Appalachia, an organization to raise consciousness and provide service to urban Appalachians living in Over-the-Rhine.

The "Appalachian Committee" led by Frank Foster continued to meet, and in the Fall of 1972 became a subcommittee of the Cincinnati Human Relations Commission. At the same time, Louise Spiegel formed an Appalachian research committee, also under the sponsorship of the Cincinnati Human Relations Commission.

Mike Maloney, having completed his studies, returned to Cincinnati and was hired by the Cincinnati Human Relations Commission with support from the

Appalachian Fund to staff the Appalachian Committee of the Cincinnati Human Relations Commission. In December, 1972 the Appalachian Committee opened an outreach office on Vine Street just at the southern edge of the Over-the-Rhine neighborhood. Katie Brown became the first volunteer worker for the committee. Serving as secretary several days a week, she was instrumental in developing the Appalachian Committee's library and in forming a Miner's Benefit Program. Seemingly unrelated, but of equal importance, was the city's first Appalachian Festival, sponsored in 1972 by the Junior League of Cincinnati under the leadership of Diane Williams. The Appalachian Festival grew to become a major Appalachian cultural activity. Funds generated by the Festival have supported many activities on behalf of urban Appalachians.

In the spring of 1973 the Heritage Room was founded by the Appalachian Committee at Washington Park School and in the summer the first urban Appalachian women's organization, the Appalachian Women's Organization was formed. Through the efforts of Mike Maloney, the City of Cincinnati agreed to include Appalachians in its Affirmative Action policy statement. This was an important accomplishment since it was the first official recognition of Appalachians as a legitimate minority population.

By early 1974, the Appalachian Committee had grown in size and influence to the point where it could stand as an independent organization. In February, the Committee assumed the charter of the Appalachian Identity Center, expanded its Board membership, and became the Urban Appalachian Council (UAC). The new organization continued to carry out the programs developed by the Appalachian Committee and the Identity Center. Initial financial support came from the Cincinnati Human Relations Commission, the Appalachian Fund, the Greater Cincinnati Foundation, and the Community Commitment Foundation. The objectives of the Urban Appalachian Council were to:

1. establish a program of research to document the needs and problems of Appalachians in Cincinnati and the gaps in services and other resources;
2. formalize a structure for helping urban professional workers to become more sensitive to the needs of Appalachians;
3. use documented evidence and other resources to urge policy-making officials and administrators to make changes in their programs in order to better serve Appalachians and others;
4. improve the urban migrants' self-image and to attack stereotypes by establishing programs to help Appalachians establish their culture;
5. promote efforts to organize Appalachian neighborhoods;
6. establish a resource center which would make both cultural and social planning information on mountain migrants accessible; and
7. establish programs at local universities that would make university resources and greater community resources available to Appalachians and other people on campus (Urban Appalachian Council, 1979).

The mid-1970's must be considered a period of great success and accomplishment for the urban Appalachian movement. UAC Executive Director Mike Maloney published the *Social Areas of Cincinnati Report* in 1974, which had significant influence on the planning done by human service agencies in Cincinnati (Maloney 1974).

A new Appalachian Heritage Room designed to serve the community was established across the street from Washington Park School. Under the sponsorship of the Battelle Institute, the first national research conference on urban Appalachians was held in Columbus, Ohio.

In 1975, the Appalachian Community Development Association was formed to assume "community control" of the Appalachian Festival. In July, 1975, the first of three summer institutes on urban Appalachians co-sponsored by the University of Cincinnati and UAC was funded by the Ohio Board of Regents. Also in the summer of 1975, Larry Reddin was hired as the first UAC worker to work in the Camp Washington and Northside neighborhoods. The following year, *Mountain Life and Work* (1976) devoted a special issue to urban Appalachians by highlighting the work of UAC.

By 1976, the Urban Appalachian Council had become a full-fledged service and advocacy agency for Appalachians in Cincinnati. The Cincinnati Human Relations Commission had ceased providing financial support for the Director's salary, and UAC developed a purchase of services agreement with the Cincinnati Community Chest. The Council also started to diversify its efforts by extending its focus to several neighborhoods in addition to Over-the-Rhine. Although the attempts at community organizing outside of the Over-the-Rhine area were a natural step in the progress of the UAC, the efforts caused clouds on the horizon that foretold the storm that was coming.

Expansion of the urban Appalachian movement caused two issues to arise. One was related to an original goal of the United Appalachians of Cincinnati, "to promote the self-awareness and self-identity" of Appalachians in Cincinnati. This identity model was central to the history and philosophy of the urban Appalachian movement. Many people involved in the work in the 1960's had been trained by Ernie Mynatt. Many of the early activities were supported or not supported, based on whether they were consistent with Mynatt's philosophy and methods. Several people believed the identity model, which was the basis for the Appalachian Identity Center, would not work in other communities. A second critical issue was how to involve new people, particularly non-Appalachians, in the movement. How could the newcomers share the early vision and appreciate the history of the urban Appalachian movement? How could the movement open itself to new concerns and maintain its original core of beliefs and philosophies?

The community organizing projects continued to expand as programs were developed and implemented in the communities of South Fairmont and Norwood. In late 1976 and early 1977, the Council received substantial new funds and staff members through an LEAA Grant for Youth Service Training, CETA, and VISTA Programs. Further, UAC and the urban Appalachian movement in Cincinnati were growing in fame and reputation. Executive Director Mike Maloney carried the urban Appalachian concerns to the national level by testifying before a Federal Task Force. This was the first federal recognition of the urban Appalachian movement. Visits to Washington would become a regular activity for the Executive Director and staff of UAC as federal agencies and the Executive branch began to show interest in and support of the urban Appalachian movement. The overall strength and influence of the organization was demonstrated by the lay role UAC played in the formation of the Inner City Neighborhood Coalition. The Coalition was successful in overturning the City of Cincinnati's "triage" policy which would have withheld support and services to "dying" inner city neighborhoods.

Despite the important accomplishments of the past several years and the promise of even greater achievement on behalf of urban Appalachians, the period from 1977 to 1982 was marked by internal organizational turmoil and strife. The growing rift between the community organizing and identity model proponents was compounded by the phenomenal growth of the staff and the involvement of a number of new individuals attracted to the movement. A second split involved the middle class professional Appalachians who wished to support the UAC and grassroots community residents. This "class" struggle was further exacerbated by an ideological difference between "those on the left and those on the right politically." The differences in philosophy, political views, and the organizational growing pains prompted the Executive Director to hire a consultant to bring harmony, a sense of direction and common commitment back to the movement. Even so, 1977 ended with the South Fairmont and Norwood Neighborhood organizations moving to become autonomous urban Appalachian organizations. The consultant's efforts resulted in the development and adoption of a new Long Range Plan for UAC. In adopting the new plan, the UAC Board announced that the original objectives of the Appalachian Committee had been achieved and that new directions were called for to benefit Appalachian migrants throughout the Midwest (Urban Appalachian Council, 1979).

The turmoil did not subside and 1978 came to be known as the "year of the conflict." Disputes over ideology and organizational philosophy resulted in the resignation of several key staff and board members over the next two years. Some of these individuals had been a part of the movement since the old coalition preceding the formation of the Urban Appalachian Council. Several continued their work on behalf of urban Appalachians by supporting the Appalachian Festival and serving on the Appalachian Community Development Association Board of Trustees. Others left to take up new endeavors.

Even with the turmoil, UAC continued to sponsor programs and extend successful efforts on behalf of Appalachian migrants. A Career Education Program was funded by CETA, a Drug Education Program was implemented, and the Urban Appalachian movement achieved recognition as a viable social movement supported by a number of agencies and organizations at the federal, state and local levels. In 1981, two major books on urban Appalachians, both the outgrowth of UAC research efforts, were published. (Philliber and McCoy, 1981; Philliber, 1981).

By 1982, however, the internal dissension and fluctuating patterns of the funding brought the organization to near collapse. The CETA and VISTA grants had been reduced and the Community Chest was threatening to discontinue its support. Mike Maloney resigned as Executive Director, along with several board members. The individual hired to replace Maloney did not complete a probationary period and was replaced by Maureen Sullivan, a former president of the UCA Board. Shortly after Sullivan's appointment, the board decided to end all CETA/JTPA funding. At the same time, although unrelated to the problems, the Identity Center was closed.

The 1983 to 1985 period is one characterized as a return to "original values."

Under Sullivan, the board and staff were reorganized and attempts were made to reestablish several programs. Ties were developed with community schools in urban Appalachian communities and a Client Advocate program begun. The reorganized UAC had regained credibility in the community and the Community Chest and City Council moved to reinstate funding.

The Urban Appalachian Council serves today as the centerpiece of an organizational network that includes several "storefront" educational centers, neighborhood-based social service centers, and two inner-city identity centers. In cooperation with the Urban Office of the Appalachian People's Service Organization and a community organizing agency called Working in Neighborhoods, the Urban Appalachian Council sponsors the Appalachian Issues Network, a coalition of five low-income Appalachian neighborhoods. Through its Frank Foster Library on Appalachian Migrants and its staff and volunteer resources, UAC sponsors or supports a broad variety of cultural activities, such as neighborhood festivals and workshops for teachers, church leaders, and all types of professional workers.

UAC maintains ties with other rural and urban Appalachian organizations through its relationship with such organizations as the Appalachian Development Projects Assembly of the Commission on Religion in Appalachia, the Council of the Southern Mountains, and the Appalachian Alliance.

Perhaps the greatest success of the urban Appalachian identity movement spearheaded by UAC is illustrated by this volume. UAC Research Committee members or former members have participated in the Appalachian Studies Conference and in conferences in the various disciplines, such as regional and national conferences of sociologists and anthropologists.

UAC's research and cultural activities have made Cincinnati a major center of the larger Appalachian movement. Its success in empowering of the poor through community organization and in developing a positive Appalachian identity has, to a certain extent, been replicated in other Ohio cities such as Dayton, Hamilton, Columbus, and Cleveland.

Dayton, Ohio is the second most important center of Appalachian cultural and political activity. Our Common Heritage (OCH) was founded in Dayton as The Kentucky Mountain Club. Our Common Heritage, like UAC, has sponsored city-wide cultural events, has been effective in advocacy, and has multiplied its efforts through spinoff organizations and influence on other agencies. Partially through the efforts of OCH, Dayton has also become a major center of Appalachian culture. Much of that cultural activity is promoted by OCH "spinoffs," the 1500-member Ohio-Kentucky-Indiana Bluegrass Association and City Folk, a multi-ethnic arts organization.

The Hamilton (Ohio) Appalachian People's Service Organization (HAPSO) owns its own building and operates a program of community organization, advocacy, cultural affirmation, and service, primarily in the North End. HAPSO received national press coverage for its successful efforts to force cleanup of the Chem-Dyne industrial site, a major hazardous waste site in the middle of the city. Like UAC and OCH, HAPSO also sponsors cultural programs such as arts and crafts festivals.

In Columbus, Ohio, the Central Ohio Appalachian Council flourished briefly around 1976 and 1977. It failed through the inability of initial leadership, primarily professional, to agree on goals and methods, and its demise was a severe setback to

UAC's effort to promote a statewide network. While it functioned, this organization illustrated the importance of having an organization in the state capitol. The initiative for legislative action to form an Ohio State Appalachian Commission came from the Central Ohio group.

From about 1970 to 1972, Appalachians in Cleveland were organized by the Appalachian Action Council, which helped establish the first urban Appalachian library. It folded when its leaders withdrew because they felt that United Way and university-based professionals had taken over the organization.

When one reviews the thirty-year history of the urban Appalachian movement, one cannot but be impressed. Appalachians in Cincinnati, with the help of many allies, successfully organized an urban social movement which has become a positive force in the life of the Greater Cincinnati community. The movement has a significant record of accomplishment and there has been a true gain in the quality of life for many Appalachian migrants living in Cincinnati and other urban areas. But at the same time there is a nagging sense of work undone, and that there are too few tomorrows left in which to do it. There is a need to renew efforts and restore to the movement the commitment of the individuals who worked so diligently in the 1950's, 1960's and 1970's. In many urban neighborhoods, Appalachian migrants continue to be displaced persons. Their children, having lost faith in themselves and respect for their heritage, are seeking a life in the streets. Honesty, independence, pride, and a sense of place, the essence of Appalachian heritage, are being lost to the hard, grab-what-you-can, values of the city. By the turn of the century, another generation of urban Appalachians will have grown up in the streets resenting their heritage and the city that destroyed it. Perhaps their ability to survive in the urban community will be greater than their parents', but they will have paid a high price. They will have lost their heritage; a loss that affects all of society.

A DECADE IN REVIEW

The Development of the Ethnic Model in Urban Appalachian Studies

Michael E. Maloney

The purpose of this paper is to review the principal developments in research relating to urban Appalachians since 1974, when the first national conference on urban Appalachians was held in Columbus, Ohio.

In the spring of 1974 a national conference on urban Appalachians was sponsored by the Academy for Contemporary Problems in Columbus, Ohio. The primary purpose of that conference was to bring together and focus the existing body of information on urban Appalachians. Grace Leybourne and Roscoe Giffin had done early research in Cincinnati, and James Brown of the University of Kentucky had collected facts and developed a theory concerning "the Great Migration." In 1971, Brown and his associates had published the landmark *Mountain Families in Transition.* Clyde McCoy, Gary Fowler, Larry Morgan, Brady Deaton, Kurt Anschell, and other students and colleagues of Brown's published research regarding Appalachian migration and adjustment. In a project commissioned by the Office of Economic Opportunity, Abt Associates had published its findings on the causes of rural-to-urban migration among the poor. Robert Coles had written vivid descriptions of Appalachian migrants in *The South Goes North.* Griffin and Hollander had published *Uptown: Poor Whites in Chicago.* *Mountain Life and Work* and *People's Appalachia* had published special issues on urban Appalachians.

From the Appalachian Committee office and the Cincinnati Human Relations Commission came *The Social Areas of Cincinnati,* which introduced the neighborhood and census tract as units of analysis to students of urban Appalachians. Thomas Wagner's dissertation study focused on the plight of Appalachians in the public schools. Staff members of the Urban Appalachian Council and faculty members from the University of Cincinnati and Northern Kentucky University began a series of working papers, which focused on school and neighborhood issues or analyzed special census-bureau data on 1965-1970 migrants to the Cincinnati metropolitan area.

Much of this work (and some not mentioned here) is summarized in *The Invisible Minority*, which grew out of the Columbus conference.

In the concluding chapter of *The Invisible Minority*, this author summarized the state of knowledge in 1974 and the need for further research as follows:

> The conclusion is that we still do not know all that we need to know. Most of our data in these studies are based on surveys of recent migrants. The peak period of Appalachian migration was the 1940's and the early 1950's. We still lack a comprehensive survey that includes the people who migrated before 1955 and their descendants. I am convinced that when such data become available, they will show that a large percentage of first- and second-generation Appalachians still live in central-city low-status areas and that, in some cases, the status of the second generation will be lower than that of the first generation. Another important characteristic of the needed studies should be that they compare Appalachians to other groups. A base of information is being developed for instance, showing that the status of Cincinnati's white Appalachian population is comparable to that of the black population. (Maloney, 1981:171)

Another challenge to future research was posed in Phillip Obermiller's article in *The Invisible Minority* :

> We must begin to look at Appalachian success patterns and social competence, and not just the social disorganization that is present within some segments of the Appalachian community. . .We should begin therefore to examine those instances in which the system has been exploited by Appalachians, and look for patterns of success which can be reinforced by policy and planning decisions. Research. . . should take into consideration the concept of neighborhood. . . Information is urgently needed on the present situation of the Appalachian family. (Obermiller, 1981:18)

In their article "Stereotypes of Appalachian Migrants," McCoy and Watkins, (1981) issue a similar call to rid ourselves of "an unbalanced and distorted image," which emphasizes the evils of the city and projects a view of all Appalachian migrants as "maladjusted and malcontented." They suggest that research be directed toward replacing these "mythical" images with facts and role models that permit the development of a positive Appalachian identity.

We can summarize the concern of the contributors to *The Invisible Minority* in this way: that exclusive focus on the social problems of urban Appalachians would lead to blaming the victim and to policies and plans that ignore the self-help capacity of family, church, and neighborhood, and to continued projection onto Appalachians and others of a negative image lacking in positive role models. In the opposite direction, some contributors were concerned that continued reliance on census data on recent migrants would paint such a rosy picture that the realities of poverty and related social conditions would be ignored.

The Development of Urban Appalachian Research: 1975-1984

Urban Appalachian research responded, at least in part, to the challenges issued in *The Invisible Minority*. Multigenerational research has been conducted in Cincinnati, though not in other cities. Researchers and practitioners have been ·more careful to emphasize the achievements of the majority of Appalachians, who are employed and have a relatively stable family and community life. Research on the family, neighborhood, church, and other social institutions has made steady progress though few ethnographies have been produced. Research and popular writing oriented toward positive Appalachian identity and role models is very limited.

An annotated bibliography of research on urban Appalachians distributed by the Urban Appalachian Council enables us to make some generalizations about the scope and extent of research during the past decade. Of a total of 172 entries in the UAC bibliography, 77 have publication dates later than March 1974. These include two hardbound books and several articles in hardbound anthologies, several softbound books, nine Ph.D. dissertations, one Congressional report, several special issues of magazines, and a broad array of working papers, research bulletins, and other types of publication.

Although more publications still focus on Cincinnati than on any other city, the geographic range is gradually broadening. Studies now exist that focus on Northern Kentucky, Clermont County, Hamilton, Dayton, Columbus, Akron, Cleveland, Toledo, Chicago, Lexington, and Baltimore.

The topics covered include various aspects of migration (6), culture (6), education (8), family (3), neighborhood (3), women (4), policy (4), health (3), religion (3), stereotypes (3), ethnicity (8), poverty (3), housing (1), the elderly (1), youth (1), black Appalachians (2), and demographic studies (9). These classifications are somewhat misleading; more than six publications focused on culture, for example, but some are not counted because they have some other primary classification. Even so, these statistics indicate some general trends.

Demographic studies, ethnicity, education, migration, and culture received more attention than housing, youth, and the elderly. Women's studies are emerging, and return migration is still a relatively undeveloped field of study.

The First Multigenerational Study

In 1975 the Cincinnati Area Project completed the first multigenerational survey research on urban Appalachians. In the succeeding nine years, the Urban Appalachian Council has made substantial use of the results of this study in its advocacy work. Since 1981, the full study has been available in a hardbound book, *Appalachian Migrants in Urban America*, by William Philliber.

Philliber's study provided answers to a broad array of questions, and in doing so it compared first- with second-generation Appalachians and white Appalachians with blacks, white natives, and migrants from other areas. The results addressed those who were concerned about the perpetuation of the poverty stereotype as well as those who were concerned that the realities of poverty, socioeconomic status, and individual and community health were underplayed.

The true picture was mixed. As this author had predicted, the Philliber study showed a substantial rate of downward mobility among second-generation Appalachians. The study also concluded that social participation tended to be limited to labor unions, that most Appalachians in Hamilton County were employed in semiskilled or unskilled jobs, and that Appalachians lagged behind white native Cincinnatians in educational and occupational attainments.

Philliber concluded that Appalachians have low levels of attainment in education, occupation, and income not because their cultural values and family structure are unadaptable to the urban environment, but because they belong to families of lower socioeconomic status, come from rural areas, and value traditionalism, all of which result in fewer years of educational attainment.

> Fewer years of education combined with lower (SES) family origins and rural backgrounds, in turn result in lower occupational attainment plus the fact that wives are less likely to participate in the labor force result in lower family income. (Philliber, 1981:87)

Philliber challenges the poverty stereotype and the victim-blaming approach with his conclusion that Appalachians are heavily suburbanized and that their values are not radically different from other groups. His research has effectively countered the belief that all Appalachians are clustered in inner-city "ports of entry" and are trapped in a cultural system that causes failure. In opposition to the welfare-malingerer stereotype, he found that only 20 percent of the sample were currently on welfare and that 55 percent had never received welfare.

In the area of physical and mental health Philliber found that Appalachians suffer more from family difficulties and personal stress than other white groups. He also found that Appalachians, unlike blacks, have a tendency to blame themselves rather than society for their problems.

Appalachians as an Urban Ethnic Group

In answer to the question, "Are Appalachians in Cincinnati an ethnic group?," Philliber concluded that Appalachians are an ethnic group in Cincinnati; they meet seven of eight major criteria for being considered an ethnic group, and lack only a unique culture. He proposes a theory that attributes to the way they have been stereotyped and denied opportunnity for advancement.

Phillip Obermiller's contribution to the question of urban Appalachians as an ethnic group began with an article in *Appalachian Journal* (5:1, Autumn, 1977). He reviewed various definitions of ethnicity and various authors' views of Appalachian ethnicity. Obermiller concluded that there is a case, though inconclusive, for considering urban Appalachians an ethnic group. His subsequent research has tended to emphasize class over ethnicity.

One of the studies reviewed in Obermiller's 1977 article was conducted by Tommie Miller (1976) among Appalachians and non-Appalachians in Norwood, Ohio. Like Philliber's 1975 study, the Miller study included first- and second-generation Appalachians. Miller concluded that others' identification of Appalachians as an ethnic group was stronger than Appalachian self-identification. Obermiller asked whether standard sociological techniques were adequate to address the question, and both Miller and Philliber stressed the need for further study. Obermiller called for the use of both value-expressive and psychological indicators in such research (Obermiller, 1981:17-18).

Martin Marger (1981) offers an implicit explanation of why the question of Appalachian ethnicity has received more attention in urban than in rural Appalachian studies. ". . . Ethnic group formation in the United States and other modern societies is a *uniquely urban phenomenon* (emphasis ours), particularly as a result of voluntary migration."

Marger's central concept is that ethnicity is an "emergent" phenomenon. It can take various forms, can be created deliberately under certain ecological and political conditions, and can be weak or strong. Ethnicity, he believes, can be strong in some members of the group and weak in others. There is no clearcut path to ethnicity but the changing political and ecological forces best explain Appalachian ethnicity and will provide the sources of its political evolution. If Marger is correct, we should not conclude summarily that urban Appalachians are ethnic or not ethnic; rather, we should ask whether they are in the process of becoming an ethnic group and, if so, in what individuals or subgroups this movement is most advanced.

For urban Appalachian scholars, the question of ethnicity amounts to this: What conceptual framework do we use in studying urban Appalachians: ethnicity, race, or class? The concept of "poor whites" implies both race and class, while the concept of "working class" could imply an approach across racial and ethnic lines. The concept of "Appalachian" ethnicity has been used for a combination of pragmatic and philosophical reasons too complex to discuss here, and the concept of "minority group" has also been used by Appalachian advocates. Unfortunately, the idea of minority-group status is often confused by the question of ethnicity.

The developments in research described in this paper have taken place, for the most part, without major government or foundation support. The scholars, practitioners, and community volunteers who have conducted efforts with and for urban Appalachians are to be commended for their hard work and creativity during the past decade. They have shown how scholarship and social practice can be linked in efforts to document the needs of a minority group and to develop programs to meet some of those needs.

3

APPALACHIANS
IN MIDWESTERN CITIES:

Regionalism as a Basis of Ethnic Group Formation

William W. Philliber & Phillip J. Obermiller

The purpose of this paper is to analyze the experiences of Appalachian migrants from the perspective of political economy theory. Evidence from a number of studies conducted over the past few years will be brought together to demonstrate the ability of this approach to recognize the emergence of Appalachians as an ethnic group in Midwestern cities.

Political economy theories see ethnic groups forming as a reaction to discrimination from more powerful groups. When the supply of the labor force exceeds the supply of available jobs, competition for those jobs is inevitable. The more the supply of labor exceeds the supply of jobs, the greater that competition will be. In order to reduce the competition to their own advantage, more powerful groups seek to establish discrimination against less powerful groups. Discrimination ensures that members of the dominant group will be first in the choice to fill available jobs. Members of groups discriminated against fill less desirable jobs or become unemployed when the supply of jobs is exhausted. A collection of people who are labeled by others as members of a common group and discriminated against because of that identification begin to identify with one another and to develop patterns of interrelationships and behaviors which are the distinguishing marks of ethnic groups (Bonacich, 1972; Hechter, 1974; Philliber, 1981).

Between 1950 and 1970 a net shift of more than three million people left the Appalachian region, most moving to cities in the Midwest (McCoy and Brown, 1981). During this period large numbers of southern blacks migrated to those same cities. But the industrial base in the region receiving large numbers of migrants had already begun to decline. The native population faced increased competition with one another because of the declining growth in jobs and further pressure from Appalachians and Southern blacks entering the Midwest in search of jobs. The situation was conducive to discrimination against Appalachians whose reaction would result in the development of a new ethnic group.

Among the early attempts to document discrimination against Appalachian migrants was McCoy and Watkins' (1981) collection of ethnic jokes told about Appalachians in Midwestern cities. Ethnic jokes imply some negative feature about members of a group, i.e. they are seen as lazy, ignorant, shiftless, uncultured, or what have you. Jokes function to spread stereotypes and to reinforce them by emphasizing negative images about the group in question. McCoy and Watkins were able to demonstrate that Appalachians are frequently the target of ethnic jokes which are well known and often repeated among the native population in the receiving cities. Politicians and celebrities alike feel free to engage in such humor to obtain a favorable reaction from native audiences. It would appear that the number of ethnic jokes is limited since the jokes told about Appalachians are told about other ethnic groups as well. Members of dominant groups merely change the butt of the joke to whichever group they are in competition with. The humor of the dominant groups where Appalachians migrated thus establishes and supports images about the unsuitability or inherent inferiority of Appalachians.

Obermiller (1982) documents the extent and nature of labeling of Appalachian migrants. He finds that the strongest negative images of Appalachians are held by middle class persons of Appalachian origin and by working class whites who are not from Appalachia. The strong negative images of Appalachians held by higher class persons of Appalachian origin suggest that many Appalachians who obtain higher status pass into the mainstream and reject an Appalachian identity. To be identified as an Appalachian could make them vulnerable to discrimination threatening the loss of their middle class status. They may maintain some interest in Appalachian artifacts by doing such things as attending festivals or collecting quilts, but they take care to separate themselves from the type of people about whom ethnic jokes are told. Working class whites who are not from Appalachia are in most direct competition with Appalachian migrants for jobs and income, and therefore stand to benefit most from discrimination against Appalachians. For that reason, they also express strong anti-Appalachian sentiment.

That discrimination results against Appalachians in Midwestern cities is documented in Philliber's (1981) study of the socioeconomic attainment process of Appalachians in Cincinnati. Appalachians who had college educations and came from middle class homes did as well in the competition for jobs and income as did others. However, Appalachians without those resources did less well than either natives to the area or migrants from other places. Discrimination against Appalachians in the working class was fairly intense. College education is a scarce resource in an industrialized society; those who obtain it are often able to convert it into jobs and income irrespective of their place of origin. Those without college educations (which includes almost all Appalachians living in the Midwest) must compete for those jobs which remain. Philliber's data indicate that the best of those jobs go to white natives or to non-Appalachian migrants with Appalachians hired next. Whatever jobs remain are then available to blacks.

When the key indicators of educational attainment, occupational status, and income are combined to form a socioeconomic index for residents in the Cincinnati area, the situation of highly stereotyped cultural and racial minorities becomes clear. Important differences exist between non-Appalachian whites, Appalachians, and blacks in both the high status and the low status categories. Appalachians are almost twice as likely and blacks are over three times as likely to be of low socioeconomic status than are non-Appalachian whites. Conversely, close to half of the non-Appalachian whites are of high socioeconomic status while the same is true of less than a third of the Appalachians and only a fifth of the blacks. It is clear that in terms of schooling, work, and earnings blacks are much worse off than the other two groups. Appalachians are faring better than blacks but worse than their non-Appalachian white counterparts. Other residents of the area are significantly better off than either blacks or Appalachians (Community Chest and Council of the Cincinnati Area, 1983).

Philliber goes on to demonstrate the development of patterns of association among Appalachians which isolate them further from the mainstream. They were found to live in predominantly Appalachian neighborhoods, to disproportionately choose other Appalachians as marital partners, and to associate with one another in predominantly Appalachian organizations such as fundamentalist Protestant churches. When given a choice, they did not frequently associate with people of other heritages.

Finally, research findings suggest that people who moved from Appalachia identify with one another and recognize themselves as an ethnic group. Miller's (1976) study of Appalachian identification in Norwood, Ohio, found that over a third of those with Appalachian backgrounds believed that Appalachians were an ethnic group and almost as many identified themselves as members of that group. While Philliber (1983) and Obermiller (1982) found lower levels of in-group identification, Appalachian identification is found to be stronger among Appalachian migrants who are not middle class, supporting the economic basis of the emergence of Appalachian ethnicity.

Theories based on cultural conflict have most often been used to explain the experiences of Appalachian migrants as well as the experiences of other minority groups. However, Philliber's study demonstrates the failure of cultural conflict explanations. In brief, his findings show that (1) cultural behaviors and values supposedly characteristic of Appalachians are not more common among Appalachians than among other groups, and (2) people who have those values and behaviors do not do less well than others in the competition for jobs and income. Appalachians were not more family oriented, more independent, more fearful of institutions, or more fatalistic. They were slightly more traditionalistic, but none of these variables were found to affect occupational or income attainment.

The findings are most consistent with a political economy approach to understanding ethnic group formation. Midwestern cities have been areas where competition for jobs and income is severe. Appalachians have been stereotyped in those cities as unsuitable in comparison to native whites or white migrants from other places. The stereotypes are particularly virulent among those people who benefit most directly from discrimination against Appalachians. That such discrimination exists is demonstrated in the attainment of jobs and income: among people without college educations and middle class origins, Appalachians do not acquire jobs and income equal to other whites. Neither cultural differences nor migrant status account for this difference. The most plausible explanation is that Appalachians are excluded in order to reduce the competition for native whites.

The reaction of working class Appalachians to this discrimination is resulting in the formation of Appalachians as an urban ethnic group. They have already established patterns of interaction which bring them together with one another and isolate them from non-Appalachians. In-group identification has developed to a level which is comparable with what is found among other ethnic groups. They are brought together not so much by common cultural bonds as by common subjection to discrimination.

URBAN APPALACHIANS AND CANADIAN MARITIME MIGRANTS:

Comparative Study of Emergent Ethnicity*

Martin N. Marger & Phillip J. Obermiller

Studies of North American ethnic groups have generally concentrated on the conditions and processes which contribute to either their endurance or decline over several immigrant generations. By contrast, little focus has been placed on their structural emergence and development. Our purpose in this paper is to investigate the processes of ethnic group formation, or what we will refer to as ethnicization, as they apply to two internal migrant groups, Appalachians in the United States and Maritimers in Canada. These two groups display key social similarities despite their distinct societal contexts and may be seen as appropriate comparative cases to shed light on the social conditions which give rise to, or impede, the development of ethnicity.

In looking at the processes of ethnicization two assumptions are made. First, ethnicity is not a constant or uniform social experience either for individuals or for groups. Rather, it is a variant, processual, and emergent phenomenon and will therefore reveal itself in different forms and with varying degrees of intensity in different social settings. Several ingredients of ethnicity are fundamental, however, though variable from case to case. In- and out-group perceptions of a common origin and culture, and an institutional structure or community based on that perceived commonality, are the major components of ethnic groups as they have traditionally evolved in industrial societies. Not only is each component a variable, evident in a variety of combinations and degrees, but each may develop naturally through socio-historical circumstances, or may be created in basically artificial form for political or economic purposes.

Second, ethnic group formation in North America is primarily an urban phenomenon, particularly among groups which emerge as a result of voluntary migration, either internal or external.[1] It is in the heterogeneity of the city that ethnic identity and community emerge, the products of confrontation and competition amongst a variety of groups for the society's rewards – jobs, housing, education, etc. Here the interaction of collectivities and individuals of varied origins and behavioral modes leads to the development of ascriptive and voluntary identities, which in turn create in-group cohesiveness and out-group ethnic categorization. It is thus to the urban environment that we must look to investigate the processes by which ethnic groups are established and subsequently mature. We have chosen to focus on two contemporary internal migrant groups since, within their respective societies, they are cases which seem to most closely reflect the formative stages of ethnicization.

Models of Ethnicization

While the processes of ethnic group formation have been largely neglected in the literature, several theoretical approaches to these processes are implicit in most analyses of North American groups.

The most traditional model of ethnicization assumes that migrants come to the host society with particular cultural characteristics which, as an adaptive response, are gradually modified by, and fused with, traits of the society's dominant group. Particularly in the urban environment, a hybrid (i.e., ethnic) culture evolves which becomes the attractive bond around which an institutional structure is molded and sustained, and which thereby fulfills the psychological and social needs of migrants (Francis, 1976; Gordon, 1964; Handlin, 1951). The chief focus of ethnicity in this view is the collectivity's distinctive culture.

A second model emphasizes the synthesis of host and immigrant group perceptions as the basis of ethnic group formation (Barth, 1969; Sarna, 1978; Shibutani and Kwan, 1965). In this view, the host or dominant group prescribes an ethnic identity to immigrants who respond with the development of an ethnic cohesiveness, partially as a protective device and partially as a means of establishing an identity within a pluralistic environment. Ethnicity is, in this view, not a particular array of culture traits, but a form of social organization, the boundaries of which are flexible in various social contexts. Perceived cultural features may disappear with little or no damage to the continuation of ethnicity (Barth, 1969; Patterson, 1975). More simply, so long as people define themselves and/or are defined by others in ethnic terms, they constitute an ethnic group. To understand the emergence of ethnicity, it is necessary to look primarily at how group identities are formed and the manner in which persons manipulate and deal with those identities.

A third approach to ethnicization stresses the ecology of the urban environment which sets the foundation for the development of ethnic community and identity. The basic assumption is that ethnic groups are products of structural conditions which are linked to ecological processes (Hershberg, 1979; Taylor, 1979; Yancey et al., 1976). Rather than islands to which migrants gravitate on the basis of a common cultural heritage or the constraints of ascription and self-awareness, ethnic groups crystallize in response to fluid urban conditions such as changing industrial bases, housing, and transportation patterns. These conditions subsequently produce varying degrees of group cohesion by creating common life styles, work relationships and voluntary associations. Such cohesion in turn leads to ethnic community and identity. Ethnic collectives, in this view, are not cultural or ascriptive constraints, but emergent units, subject to different developmental patterns in a variety of ecological circumstances.

Finally, ethnicization, particularly in contemporary societies, has been viewed as the product of the organizational efforts of collectivities to secure a greater share of the society's rewards. Most simply, ethnic groups are political interest or solidary groups, comprised of individuals who share common economic and social concerns; and who therefore, cohere in response to competition from other groups (Bell, 1975; Cohen, 1969; Glazer and Moynihan, 1970; 1975; Lyman and Douglass, 1973). Cultural symbols, in this view, are important only as demarcating mechanisms among competing groups.

None of these models is by itself sufficiently inclusive to constitute a complete explanation of ethnic group formation; rather, they are partial and complementary approaches, highlighting particular variables that must be viewed in different combinations. Despite their inter-dependence, however each model emphasizes a set of factors which may prove more vital in the developmental stages of ethnicization for particular groups which exhibit varying degrees of cultural and identificational clarity. Moreover, one or the other of them has been favored by social scientists. The latter three models have been generally preferred in recent years while the cultural model has been de-emphasized.

In the remainder of this paper we will outline the social characteristics and experiences of Appalachian migrants in the United States and migrants from the Atlantic provinces in Canada, using these models as a framework in which to analyze the extent and nature of ethnic development among them. We will conclude with a discussion of some of the theoretical and empirical questions which are prompted by our comparison of the two groups and the extent to which these models are supported by our analysis.

Migrant Appalachians and Maritimers

The value of comparative social analysis lies in the opportunity to move beyond individual case studies and to hypothesize on the basis of recurrent and parallel patterns within divergent social settings. The comparative approach is of even greater utility when groups in different societies, displaying generally similar social characteristics, may be placed side by side. Migrants from the Southern Appalachian region to cities of the American Midwest and from the Atlantic provinces of Canada to cities of Ontario provide such a comparative case. Much of our description will focus specifically on migrants in the receiving communities of Cincinnati and Toronto, but patterns evident in these cities are assumed to be generally prevalent in comparable cities of the two regions. Let us briefly delineate the common characteristics and social settings of these two groups.

The process of ethnic group formation necessarily begins with a migratory movement from one society or, in the case of internal migrants, from one region to another. The push-and-pull factors of migration and the regions of origin of these two groups are closely analogous. The Atlantic, or Maritime provinces of Canada – Nova Scotia, New Brunswick, Prince Edward Island, and Newfoundland – traditionally have been economically backward and depressed by comparison with other provinces.[2] The region is typified by rural non-farm communities, a large proportion tied to the fishing industry. In addition to fishing, extractive industries, particularly mining and lumbering, characterize the economies of three of the four provinces. Net outmigration has been characteristic of the region since the late nineteenth century, prompted traditionally by the decline of small farming and the mechanization of extractive and fishing industries. For example, employment in the coal mines of Nova Scotia declined from 13,500 in 1940 to 10,000 in 1955, and to 7500 in 1959 (Dasgupta, 1975). Farming, though ordinarily of the subsistence type, has also declined, thereby channeling more people into out-migration streams.

Migration streams in Canada flow primarily westward. The Atlantic provinces send their out-migrants principally to Ontario, by-passing the adjacent province of Quebec (George, 1970; Stone, 1969). In the post-World War II era, Ontario has been the industrial heartland of Canada, thus offering the most job opportunities for relatively low-skilled workers. Though net out-migration from the Atlantic provinces has been evident throughout the twentieth century (McDonald, 1968; Levitt, 1960; Stone, 1969), it reached its peak in the early 1960's. This movement coincides with markedly high unemployment rates in the region during these years.

The Southern Appalachian region includes the mountainous portions of Alabama, Georgia, Tennessee, North Carolina, Kentucky, Virginia, and all of West Virginia. Extractive industries, specifically coal mining, have been the region's chief economic base, although some textile manufacturing, timbering and farming can also be found. The forces impelling out-migration from the Southern Appalachian region of the U.S. are similar to those affecting migration from the Atlantic provinces of Canada. Push factors include the residual effects of the Great Depression and World War II.

Between 1940 and 1970, the Southern Appalachian region lost over three million persons through net out-migration; half of this loss occurred during the period between 1950 and 1960 (McCoy and Brown, 1981). Of the top fifteen receiving cities for Appalachian migrants between 1955 and 1960, six were major midwestern metropolises such as Cincinnati. In short, out-migration from Appalachia and the Atlantic provinces has followed the customary pattern of most migratory movements: a surplus population in an economically depressed area seeks ecomonic betterment through migration to a society or region which promises improved conditions.

In addition to the similarity of migration and region of origin, both groups display strikingly similar characteristics of age, race, religion, language, and social class. Both migrant populations are relatively young (Levitt, 1960; Brown and Hillery, 1962), heavily Protestant (Steeves, 1964; Brewer, 1962), white and English-speaking.[3]

As to social class, the majority of both Appalachians and Maritimers are working class, specifically unskilled or semi-skilled blue-collar workers. Educationally, both migrant groups are below the national and state (for Maritimers, provincial) averages (Steeves, 1964, Wagner 1973). The general class profile of the Appalachian migrant to Cincinnati and the Maritime migrant to Toronto is an under-educated, unskilled blue-collar worker.

Once they enter the urban environment, Appalachian and Maritime migrants may be further subdivided into two class elements. One comprises those individuals who make a rapid adjustment to the city, find steady employment, establish residence in a working-class suburban community and are quietly absorbed into the dominant group. The other subset is comprised of those who do not find stable work, remain in low-income, transitional neighborhoods and eventually come to the attention of welfare, police, and other community agencies, and, ultimately, the community at large. It is the latter element of the migrant that becomes the referent of negative group stereotypes and out-group recognition in general.

Emergent Ethnicity Within the Two Groups

THE CULTURAL MODEL. Both Maritimers in Toronto and Appalachians in Cincinnati bring elements of a common regional culture to the city, but elements which *in toto* do not sharply set them off from other groups. The parameters of Appalachian culture have been widely discussed (Billings, 1974; Erickson, 1976; Fischer, 1983; Ford, 1962; Philliber, 1981), but many of its outstanding features are characteristic of a wide spectrum of American social groups, and are commonly attributed to working and lower-class groups in general.[4] Similarly, Maritimers lack culture traits sufficiently different to set them apart from the dominant Anglo-Saxon group in Toronto.

Their lack of cultural distinctness has impeded the development of ethnic community for both groups. Breton (1964) posits that when an ethnic group displays great differences from the host community, institutional self-sufficiency is likely to develop within the group. Ethnic communities may range from those which are institutionally complete, wherein individuals need make no use of the host society's institutions, to those which are almost entirely institutionally incomplete, wherein the network of interpersonal relations is almost totally within the context of the host society. Both urban Appalachians and Maritimers presently seem very close to the latter extreme. Almost all needs of social life are met primarily within and through institutions of the host or dominant group. For both groups, then, the cultural factor appears to be a weak component in the emergence of ethnicity.

THE ETHNIC BOUNDARY MODEL. At present, there is lacking any solid data base through which the extent of ethnic self-perception among Maritimers in Toronto might be deduced. We may reasonably conclude, however, that, given their relatively weak institutional structure and lack of political mobilization, such group awareness remains slight.[5]

Among urban Appalachians, ethnic identity has been little studied, but a few preliminary investigations indicate a relatively weak ethnic self-perception (Miller, 1976; Obermiller, 1982; Philliber, 1981; Traina, 1980). Organizations in the city with an explicit Appalachian self-consciousness are small and relatively few in number, given the size of the Appalachian population in the metropolitan area.

The development and maintenance of ethnic boundaries, however, are not simply dependent on individual choice but also, and perhaps more fundamentally, on out-group perception and categorization. The extent of out-group identification of Maritimers in Toronto is largely unmeasured, but there is at least some evidence to confirm the application of negative stereotypes. This is particularly the case for Newfoundlanders, though migrants from the Atlantic provinces are frequently viewed in the aggregate. This largely negative "Newfie" stereotype is prevalent among Canadians generally (Anderson and Frideres, 1981). Indeed, "Newfie" jokes, suggesting the innate lack of intelligence of Newfoundlanders, constitute a common form of Canadian ethnic humor.

Out-group recognition of Appalachians in Cincinnati is primarily of two types. Positive aspects of Appalachian life are presented on a city-wide basis by acceptance of Appalachian culture. However, negative stereotypes of Appalachians abound in the media, popular and scholarly literature, in various marketing devices, and in the common lore of the city (McCoy and Watkins, 1981). While the emblematic term "Appalachian" is not widely used or accepted, stigmatic epithets such as "hillbilly," "briar-hopper," and "ridgerunner" are frequently used to label anyone speaking with a southern accent.

THE ECOLOGICAL MODEL. While the cultural and ethnic boundary models of ethnicization seem to yield only fractional manifestations of emergent ethnicity among either urban Appalachians or Maritimers, urban ecological patterns provide more substantial evidence of ethnic group formation, particularly for Appalachians.

While Atlantic migrants in Toronto and other Ontario cities collectively occupy mainly lower-level blue collar positions, they are not concentrated exclusively, or even generally, in any particular industry. Their position in the occupational hierarchy is shared with members of first-generation European, Asian, and West Indian immigrant groups in the city. As well, the relatively diversified industrial base of Toronto makes for a dispersal of blue-collar workers in many industries.

Urban Appalachians in Cincinnati and other cities of the lower Midwest, by contrast, are more clearly concentrated in particular industries requiring large semi- and unskilled labor forces, such as automobile production. These have traditionally served as prime occupational areas for migrant Appalachians since large-scale in-migration began in the 1940's. Moreover, in Cincinnati, the chief rivals for such jobs are not first-, or even, second-, generation immigrants, but blacks, who represent another internal migrant group, one even less skilled and traditionally subject to more customary and institutionalized discrimination (Philliber and Obermiller 1982).

Patterns of residential clustering are also clear for Appalachians in Cincinnati, and moderately evident for Maritimers in Toronto. Residential clustering among Appalachians well into the second migrant generation in Cincinnati and other Midwestern cities has been well documented (Davies and Fowler, 1972; Fowler and Davies, 1972; Henderson, 1966; Hyland, 1970; Killian, 1970; McKee and Obermiller, 1978; Peterson et al., 1977; Schwarzweller et al, 1971). Their concentration in low-skilled occupations has created Appalachian working-class enclaves in Cincinnati and its surrounding area where large manufacturing industries are located. Appalachian patterns of residence in the city are thus the product not simply of social congruity but of urban ecology (Philliber, 1981). In this, Appalachians have followed patterns not unlike those of earlier immigrant groups in American cities (Hershberg, 1979; Ward, 1971).

In Toronto, city-wide surveys, census data and other municipal records do not include items concerning province of origin. As a result, patterns of residence for migrant Maritimers are undocumented. Moreover, since they are English-speaking, Maritimers are not identifiable by mother tongue as are other Toronto ethnic groups. In addition, the fact that upwardly mobile maritimers are quickly and silently absorbed into the dominant group makes it difficult to ascertain the residential patterns of this grouping. Nonetheless, certain areas of metropolitan Toronto are recognized for their sizable element of Maritimers. Basically, two types of residential areas are evident.

One comprises the central city transitional zones which serve as port-of-entry for most, but which are relatively quickly abandoned by those who acquire steady employment. Some do remain, however, but share these areas with the lower-class segment of other urban groups. The other type is the working-class suburb which contains the bulk of Toronto's heavier manufacturing enterprises.

THE POLITICAL MODEL. Although the potential for political ethnicity seems to be in place for both urban Appalachians and Maritimers, in neither case has this potential been tapped to any significant degree. In the case of urban Appalachians, an incipient ethnic movement arose as part of the urban welfare and civil rights activism of the 1960's (Maloney, 1979), but it did not display the growth of other ethnic advocacy movements which evolved during that period. A few groups at the community level have continued to pursue issues relevant to the status and recognition of Appalachians in the urban area (Maloney, 1979; Neely, 1979), but their impact has not been of major proportions. Most importantly, urban Appalachians have not yet developed into a clear-cut political force, able to exert significant influence in local elections. Moreover, political leaders have not made strong efforts to court this group, despite its sizable electoral potential in Cincinnati and several other cities of the region. At best, urban Appalachians have acquired a minimal degree of recognition as a distinct constituency by government agencies and private support groups.

Maritimers in Toronto have displayed an even less obvious political presence. No appeals to this group on the part of political leaders have been made, and even welfare and educational institutions have not seen fit to create programs aimed exclusively at Maritimers. Rather, social services and programs have been rendered under the umbrella of general community services. Combined with their lack of cultural distinctness, the relatively dispersed residential pattern of the Atlantic migrants in Toronto restrains political leaders from dealing with them as a separate client group. In a sense, Maritimers have been lost in the extremely variegated ethnic mosaic of post-World War II Toronto. During this period, the city has served as one of the major points of destination for European immigrants, and much of the metropolitan area's substantial growth is attributable to foreign immigration. As a result, Toronto politicians, educators and social service agencies have been preoccupied in the past twenty years with European and, to a lesser extent, Asian and West Indian immigrant groups. These are the groups in Toronto which have displayed clear patterns of residential clustering.

This has not been the case in Cincinnati where large European ethnic communities have ceased to typify the general populace. The relatively substantial black community (one-third of the city's populace), however, has served in a somewhat similar manner to camouflage Appalachians from political leaders and social service agencies. Just as policy makers and opinion leaders in Toronto have focused their attention on more visible groups, those in Cincinnati have focused on the black community.

Discussion

Our description of Appalachian migrants in Cincinnati and Atlantic migrants in Toronto indicates that the emergence of ethnicity for either group is not firm or even entirely visible. Indeed, it might be argued that it is premature to speak in ethnic terms of groupings that lack readily distinguishable culture or physical traits, that have a minimal sense of corporate self-awareness, that have developed only the most primitive of institutional structures and that have not yet engaged seriously in collective political action. We would argue, however, that the process of ethnicization has begun for both groups to the extent that 1) each has become distinguishable on the basis of perceived group differences which have given rise to the development of out-group stereotyping, and 2) both have displayed ecological characteristics somewhat similar to those of older, solidly established urban ethnic groups that should naturally engender further group cohesiveness and an awareness of commonality of fate. In short, certain key factors are in place for these two groups which appear critical in the ethnicization process.

At the same time, however, the prognosis for the furtherance of ethnic group development among both urban Appalachians and Maritimers suggests a movement limited in scope and degree. We would assert that this is attributable primarily to these groups lack of visibility–either cultural or phenotypical–which in turn induces mobilization and the pursuit of group interests along class, rather than ethnic, lines.

The potentialities for a more complete ethnicity for either of these groups cannot lie in the engendering of group awareness based on culture, as has been the case most commonly for urban immigrant groups. Nor can the discrimination arising from physical distinction lead to a more advanced level of institutional completeness, as has been the experience of blacks and other racially-defined groups in the United States (Taylor, 1979). Given their lack of strong cultural or physical features, more advanced ethnicization for Appalachians and Maritimers lies in one or more of the following paths: 1) the strengthening of out-group recognition through the deliberate promotion and amplification of those group features already prominent; 2) the stabilization of ecological patterns; or 3) the formation of these groupings into political interest groups, or what Gamson (1968:36) calls solidary groups, that is, collections of individuals "who think in terms of the effect of political decisions on the aggregate and feel that they are in some way personally affected by what happens to the aggregate."

All of these possible courses, however, are strongly influenced by the factor of absence of visibility. As a result, class interests, community and identity tend to supersede ethnic interests, community and identity. Out-group identification, we have concluded, is well established for urban Appalachians and somewhat less so for Maritime migrants. But upward class mobility for individual members of these groups spells the demise of out-group recognition, and hence the diminishment of in-group awareness and community based on ethnic features. Since their major culture traits are already those of the dominant group, and they are not physically distinct, cultural and structural assimilation are rendered meaningless for these groups. For them, assimilation is more accurately a class, rather than an ethnic, phenomenon. Upward class mobility is a movement "up and out" instead of "up within," as is the case for the first two generations of culturally defined groups, or for an indefinite number of generations of racially-defined groups.

Likewise, given their relative lack of dissimilarity to the dominant group, ecological patterns for these groups are more critically a function of class differences, not ethnic consolidation. While cultural and physical dissimilarities may explain a great part of the residential segregation of other urban groups (see Darroch and Marston, 1971), as well as their concentration in particular occupational areas, for the most part they cannot account for the residential and occupational patterns of urban Appalachians or Maritimers.

Political development for these groups is also very much a function of class rather than ethnic interests. This is based on both external as well as internal perceptions of political interest. Since the majority of both groups remain well ensconced in the lower echelons of the working class, efforts at political mobilization must be directed primarily to this subset of the larger group. Lacking cultural or physical distinctness, these groups' ethnic interests are apt to be dismissed by external political leaders and bureaucracies who place them into more inclusive class categories (e.g., "working class" or "urban poor"). Failure to gain recognition as an ethnic unit by political elites and agencies further detracts from the creation of collective group awareness.

Internally, ethnic political mobilization requires a kind of artificially created ethnicity, based on the perception of political benefits to be derived from such a group membership. Because of weak group visibility, class interests easily displace potential ethnic interests. For both class segments of these groups – those who are regularly employed and those who are chronically under or unemployed – there is little compulsion to organize politically or to perceive community issues along ethnic lines; for them, political benefits are dispensed through comprehensive class interest groups such as labor unions or social welfare organizations.

For both urban Appalachians and Maritimers an ethnically-based political movement is not likely to be attractive since its purposes cannot speak to either their economic needs or their problems of self-definition.[6] Patterson's (1975) principle of "optimization of interest" seems appropriate to both groups. He maintains that individuals will be most intensely involved with that allegiance which is in their own best social and economic interests. Thus, where ethnicity yields a payoff, it will be stressed over class, though where the two are in conflict, class will always take precedence. In short, class interests determine the strength of ethnicity. In the case of both urban Appalachians and Maritimers, there is insufficient incentive to identify and to mobilize along ethnic rather than class lines; political action thus turns on class, not ethnic, cleavages.

The two cases we have analyzed suggest that a group's cultural and/or physical visibility is vital to the development of ethnicity; where either is lacking, ethnicity can emerge only to a limited level. Given a group's marginal perceptibility in the host society, it cannot be expected to move far beyond what Yinger (1976) has called "stereotyped" ethnicity. In such cases, there is some degree of social definition of the group in ethnic terms, but other aspects of ethnicity are essentially lacking. Class definitions of group members – both self and other – pre-empt ethnic definitions. At best, such groupings may be viewed as ethnic categories rather than ethnic collectiveness or groups (Cohen, 1969; McKay and Lewins, 1978; Williams, 1979). It may be hypothesized, then, that in cases where groups lack salient cultural or physical distinctness from the dominant group, class factors supersede ethnic factors in political mobilization, ecological patterns and, to a lesser extent, group identification.

Our analysis also suggests that ethnic group boundaries are not totally flexible.

Structuralists have argued that ethnicity is a reactive phenomenon in which group boundaries emerge in response to institutional discrimination or to negative stereotyping by out-groups. Our study suggests that factors of cultural commonality and/or physical visibility are nonetheless vital to such boundary establishment. Conceptualizations of the ethnic group which depend essentially on self- and other-identification or on the establishment of favorable ecological or political conditions are inadequate without the antecedent of a perceived common culture or physical distinction upon which some conception and consciousness of a distinction upon which those identifications and conditions are based. The experience of Appalachians and Maritimers in the urban environment supports van der Berghe's (1978:xvii) assertion that "there can be no ethnicity (or race) without some conception and consciousness of a distinction between 'them' and 'us'. But these subjective perceptions do not develop at random; they crystallize around clusters of objective characteristics that become badges of inclusion or exclusion." Although ethnic boundaries are flexible and may be essentially artificial creations of social-psychological, ecological, or political circumstances, they are nonetheless necessarily founded on a cultural and/or physical basis. There must be a perceived commonality on the part of both in-group and out-group to engender ethnic identity and community. Such a feeling of oneness ordinarily derives from the perception of a unique cultural heritage or common phenotypic traits.

NOTES

* Reprinted from *International Journal of Comparative Sociology*, 24:229-43.

1. Relatively isolated rural ethnic groups in the U.S., notably Scandinavians, as well as self-contained groups such as the Amish, are what Francis (1976) calls "primary ethnic groups." In these groups, the basic social needs of members are satisfied almost totally without direct participation in the host society. The very opposite conditions obtain for urban immigrant groups.

2. The original Maritime provinces are Nova Scotia, New Brunswick, and Prince Edward Island. Newfoundland did not enter the Canadian confederation until 1949. Since then, the four eastern provinces have generally been referred to as the Atlantic or Maritime provinces. Our references to Atlantic migrants or Maritimers are synonymous.

3. There are segments of Brunswick, where they constitute about 30 percent of the population, are French-speaking groups of any numerical significance. Because they settle mainly in Quebec rather than Ontario, Francophone migrants will not enter into our analysis. Indians, Inuit, and, in Nova Scotia, blacks, make up insignificant numbers in the region, and do not represent more than a handful of the migrant populace.

4. Although much has been written about Appalachian culture, no consensus exists as to what characteristics properly belong to the culture, or even whether such a culture exists at all.

5. A moderate corporate consciousness can be found among Newfoundlanders, due to the more distinct culture traits this subgroup displays. Some have maintained, rather exaggeratedly, that Newfoundlanders are as distinct as Italians, Greeks, or any of the European groups of the city (see for example Horwood, 1979). Though this may be an overdrawn perception, there are unquestionably certain identifying features of Newfoundlanders which serve to more sharply set them off from other groups in Toronto, as well as from other Atlantic migrants. But the intensity of both in- and out-group identification cannot be said to resemble that of other more culturally and/or physically distinct groups in the city.

6. Other impediments to political mobilization, whether encouraged internally or externally, are the proximity of the region of origin for both groups and their relatively frequent physical mobility. The two are not unrelated. Given the proximity of the regions of origin, native community ties are maintained that do not fully permit a sense of permanence among group members in the urban environment. Unlike previous immigrant groups, which essentially removed themselves from their native societies and severed their roots, urban Appalachians and Maritimers engage in a constant back-and-forth movement between old and new social settings. A psychological commitment to the new community—even after lengthy residence—is thus not complete, and inhibits political involvement.

    Political mobilization is made difficult as well by the physical mobility during the migration experience exhibited by members of both groups, particularly those who do not find steady employment. In the case of Maritimers, many are perpetual drifters who move on to other Ontario cities if they do not find suitable work in Toronto, or return to their original communities. Moreover, those who do not experience a stable employment outcome of their move to Toronto (i.e., those who remain in the transitional neighborhoods and who are clients of welfare and police authorities) are the least likely to respond to efforts at political mobilization.

5

LABELING URBAN APPALACHIANS

Phillip J. Obermiller

The boundary model of ethnic group formation has been used but never subjected to empirical investigation among Appalachian migrants (McCoy and Watkins, 1981). This model, which deals with in-group and out-group perceptions of group identity, suggests that stereotypes are among the most common markers for delineating social boundaries and therefore establishing social identities. This paper will explore the role of stereotypes in the formation of social boundaries among urban Appalachians, as well as among blacks, Appalachians, and other white residents of a large metropolitan area.

The stereotyping of rural Appalachians is a consistent phenomenon which has been documented extensively (Billings, 1974; Fisher, 1983; Ergood, 1983; Shapiro, 1978). From an urban perspective, however, little consensus is found concerning Appalachian stereotypes. Maloney and Huelsman (1972), in a review of the behavioral-science literature on Appalachian migrants, remark on the prevalence of popular stereotypes in what presents itself as scholarly writing. On the other hand, McCoy and Watkins (1981) propose that scholarship be used to debunk popular stereotypes of urban Appalachians. Some commentators interpret stereotypes of Appalachian migrants negatively as "barriers to assimilation" (Branscome, 1976:72), while others see them as positive sources of in-group cohesion and consciousness (Billings and Walls, 1980).

Lewis Killian, in writing about white southerners in Chicago, makes several important points regarding stereotypes of Appalachian migrants. He notes that "hillbilly" is an ephithet used to designate "a mountaineer, a white southerner whose caricature is to be seen in the Snuffy Smith of the comic strip" (Killian, 1970:13). Killian also points out that the "traits considered typical of white southerners were similar to those found in the stereotypes of many other minority groups" (Killian, 1970:107). These traits include racism, violence, clannishness, low standards of hygiene, laziness, and a general apathy towards education. The function of such stereotyping, according to Killian, is to justify discrimination against "hillbillies" in in urban public facilities, housing, and employment.

The Study

In general, experimental studies of the stereotyping of groups such as Appalachian migrants follow one of two methods. Either a laboratory situation is established, in which subjects are exposed to various stimuli such as pictures while researchers note their reactions, or subjects are asked to formulate or select trait-descriptive adjectives or phrases that reflect their attitude toward the object group. Katz and Braly (1933) conducted an experiment of the latter type at Princeton in 1933 which, with some modification, has been used successfully in contemporary large-scale survey research on stereotypes (Ehrlich and Rinehart, 1965; Guichard and Connolly, 1977; Kutner, 1973).

This study has modified Katz and Braly's method in several ways. It limits the number of labels being tested to fourteen, and divides them evenly between positive and negative stereotypes.[1] The stereotypes are not presented as single adjectives, but are phrased as statements, and a range of possible responses is offered.[2]

The data used in this paper were gathered in 1980 as a part of the Greater Cincinnati Survey, a RDD telephone survey. The survey involved 1,111 adult residents of Hamilton County, of whom 237 were identified as either first- or second-generation Appalachians. First-generation Appalachians were defined as anyone born in one of the 396 counties in the Appalachian region; second-generation Appalachians were defined as having at least one parent born in that area.[3] Although the survey acquired information on black Appalachians, only the data on white Appalachians were tabulated.[4]

Findings

It is essential to compare the basic social characteristics of the three groups as a preliminary step toward understanding their attitudes. Appalachians in greater Cincinnati have the same general age profile and sex distribution as blacks and non-Appalachian whites, and all three groups on the average have lived in the area approximately the same number of years. Distinct differences appear, however, when the three groups are compared for educational attainment, occupational status, and income.

Disproportionately few Appalachians (36%) and blacks (31%) have had any college experience in comparison to the non-Appalachian white population (48%). In addition, these three groups are quite distinct in occupational status. Blacks are represented disproportionately in the operative and labor/service job categories, but are underrepresented in the professional and managerial occupations in comparison to both Appalachians and non-Appalachian whites. Appalachian whites differ from their non-Appalachian counterparts primarily in the high percentage of operatives among Appalachians (19% vs. 7%) and in the relatively low percentage of Appalachians in the sales/clerical job categories (38% vs. 26%). The distribution of family income for Appalachians and for other whites in Hamilton County is quite similar, but a much higher percentage of blacks is found in the lowincome range; 46% of black families have annual incomes of less than $15,000.

In overall socioeconomic status, white Appalachians are distinct from both non-Appalachians and blacks.[5] White non-Appalachians are generally in the higher-status group, while a higher percentage of blacks is found in the low socioeconomic category. Appalachian whites fall between these two groups in their overall socioeconomic status.

This brief demographic profile of the three groups provides a context for studying the images they have of urban Appalachians. Table 5:1 presents the fourteen positive and negative stereotypes of Appalachians that were included in the study. The labels are rank ordered by the percentage of each of the three groups in agreement with the stereotypes

Each of the three groups is more positive than negative in its typification of Appalachian migrants, although, as might be expected, Appalachian whites accept more positive labels than do non-Appalachian whites or blacks. The positive labels "familistic," "religious," and "loyal" rank high among all three groups, while "apathetic," "alcoholic," and "violent" have least acceptance among Appalachian and non-Appalachian whites. Approximately three out of five people in each group agreed that Appalachians seemed to speak with a distinct accent. "Racist" was the next most widely accepted negative label. Spearman's measure, however, which was used to compare the rank ordering among the three groups shows no great diversity among the rankings.

TABLE 5:1

RANK ORDERING BY PERCENT OF AGREEMENT FOR ALL LABELS OF WHITE
APPALACHIANS CATEGORIZED BY CULTURE GROUP AND APPALACHIAN GENERATION

Rank Order	Non-Appalachian Blacks	%	Non-Appalachian Whites	%	Appalachian Whites	%	First Generation Appalachian Whites	%	Second Generation Appalachian Whites	%
1.	Familistic	69.2	Familistic	79.2	Familistic	84.0	Religious	85.3	Loyal	86.0
2.	Religious	64.8	Loyal	76.2	Loyal	83.9	Familistic	82.0	Familistic	85.2
3.	Loyal	62.4	Religious	67.9	Religious	82.0	Loyal	82.0	Independent	81.5
4.	Independent	57.4	*Accent	62.8	Independent	74.1	*Accent	67.3	Religious	77.9
5.	*Accent	57.1	Independent	62.7	*Accent	71.3	Independent	67.0	*Accent	74.7
6.	Honest	48.1	Honest	58.2	Honest	67.6	Honest	64.6	Honest	69.2
7.	Patriotic	48.0	Patriotic	54.4	Resourceful	64.3	Patriotic	64.6	Resourceful	68.7
8.	Resourceful	47.3	Resourceful	53.6	Patriotic	62.3	Resourceful	58.5	*Racist	62.7
9.	*Racist	43.7	*Racist	47.2	*Racist	57.1	*Racist	52.6	Patriotic	58.1
10.	*Apathetic	32.5	*Uneducated	47.0	*Uneducated	47.6	*Uneducated	43.0	*Uneducated	53.9
11.	*Uneducated	27.5	*Untidy	39.7	*Untidy	36.4	*Untidy	33.3	*Untidy	40.3
12.	*Alcoholic	26.2	*Apathetic	29.2	*Apathetic	27.4	*Apathetic	26.8	*Apathetic	29.1
13.	*Untidy	25.9	*Alcoholic	20.3	*Alcoholic	20.1	*Alcoholic	23.4	*Alcoholic	16.8
14.	*Violent	22.7	*Violent	16.8	*Violent	16.8	*Violent	I8.0	*Violent	13.8

*Indicates Negative Label

Important differences do exist in the amount of agreement shown for any given label. Appalachian whites have high levels of acceptance of positive labels, while non-Appalachian whites and blacks accept the same labels to a distinctly lesser degree. Appalachian and non-Appalachian whites coincide in their relative rates of agreement on only one positive label: "familistic." The black group differs significantly from the Appalachian group in relative rates of agreement on every positive label; in fact, fewer than half the black respondents agree that Appalachian whites are either "honest," "patriotic," or "resourceful." All three groups coincide in their relatively low levels of acceptance of four negative labels: "violent," "alcoholic," "apathetic," and "untidy." For the negative labels "uneducated" and "accent," however, Appalachians are much harsher in their view of themselves than are the blacks. In addition, Appalachian whites appear significantly more racist in their own eyes than in the eyes of either non-Appalachian whites or blacks.

TABLE 5:2

PERCENTAGE OF RESPONDENTS AGREEING WITH POSITIVE AND NEGATIVE LABELS
OF WHITE APPALACHIANS CATEGORIZED BY CULTURE GROUP AND GENERATION

First Generation Appalachian Whites	Second Generation Appalachian Whites	Label	Non-Appalachian Whites	Appalachian Whites	Non-Appalachian Blacks
82.0	86.0	Loyal	76.2*	83.9	62.4*
85.3	77.9	Religious	67.9*	82.0	64.8*
82.0	85.2	Familistic	79.2	84.0	69.2*
58.5	68.7	Resourceful	53.6*	64.3	47.3*
64.6	58.1	Patriotic	54.4*	62.3	48.0*
67.0*	81.5	Independent	62.7*	74.1	57.4*
64.6	69.2	Honest	58.2*	67.6	48.1*
18.0	13.8	Violent	16.8	16.7	22.7
23.4	16.8	Alcoholic	20.3	20.1	26.2
26.8	29.1	Apathetic	29.2	27.4	32.5
33.3	40.3	Untidy	39.7	36.4	25.9
43.0	53.9	Uneducated	47.0	47.6	27.5*
67.3	74.7	Accent	62.8	71.3	57.1*
52.6	62.7	Racist	47.2*	57.1	43.7*

*P < 0.05

The calculation of stereotyping scores allows for a comparison of group attitudes while controlling for selected demographic variables.[6] Table 5:3 gives the stereotyping scores for each group in the study. The raw scores indicate that, as might be expected, non-Appalachian blacks have fairly strong negative images of Appalachians, and white Appalachians have a rather strong positive attitude toward themselves; less predictably, non-Appalachian whites were found to have moderately positive images of Appalachians. Conversely, increasing socioeconomic status among non-Appalachian whites shows a marked tendency toward positive images of Appalachians while relatively little difference appears among non-Appalachian blacks of varying socioeconomic status.

TABLE 5:3: STEREOTYPING SCORES FOR THREE CULTURE GROUPS AND TWO GENERATIONS OF WHITE APPALACHIANS

Culture Group/ Generation	Positive Labels Agreed With Beyond Average Number	Score	Negative Labels Agreed With Beyond Average Number	Score	Stereotype Score
CULTURE GROUP Non-Appalachian Blacks	0	.0	3	.43	-.43
Appalachian Whites	7	1.0	4	.57	.43
Non-Appalachian Whites	3	.43	2	.29	.14
GENERATION First Generation Appalachian Whites	2	.29	2	.29	.0
Second Generation Appalachian Whites	5	.71	4	.57	.14

Discussion

The research indicates an overall preference for positive rather than negative stereotypes of Appalachian migrants. Of the three groups in the study, Appalachians showed the strongest preference for positive labels; to a lesser degree, the same can be said of non-Appalachian whites. Non-Appalachian blacks were the least accepting of positive statements about Appalachians. Acceptance of negative labels was less prevalent in all three groups but strongest among Appalachians.

Race appears to be a major factor in interpreting these results; non-Appalachian blacks are significantly less positive and only slightly less negative about Appalachians than are the two white groups. Because of the limited nature of this study, it is not possible to determine whether this response is related to Appalachians in particular or to Appalachians as members of the dominant white majority in the county.

Among the fourteen labels presented, the label "accent" was the most problematic. Although presented as a negative label, "accent" ranks fifth in percentage of agreement among the positive labels and well above the negative labels. Moreover, it correlated highly with two strong, positive labels, "familistic" and "loyal." It seems reasonable to conclude that speaking with an accent may be perceived as a positive characteristic of Appalachians.

If "accent" is removed from the list of negative labels, the two most widely accepted labels of white Appalachians are "racist" and "uneducated." Although the strongest agreement with these labels is found among Appalachians, it should be noted that more than one-fifth of the sample expressed doubts or disagreement with the most popular positive stereotype of Appalachians. Likewise, almost one-fifth of those surveyed expressed agreement with the least popular negative stereotype. From these figures it is obvious that there exists a substantial body of negative opinion regarding Appalachians.

The strongest negative labeling of white Appalachians emanates from a cohort within the Appalachian group itself. Socioeconomic stratification among the Appalachian residents of the county appears to account for an important proportion of the negative stereotypes attributed to this group. Appalachian whites with high educational attainment, white-collar occupations, and relatively high incomes are the strongest negative stereotypers of Appalachians. This pattern of intragroup stereotyping is also found among other urban minorities (Frazier, 1957; Kilson, 1983).

Assuming that they are not derogating themselves, it is reasonable to conclude that high-status Appalachians are directing these negative images toward lower-status members of their own group. This negative labeling may be attributed less to the competitive advantage gained in winning or keeping social rewards than to an effort to seek social and psychological advantage by placing distance between themselves and the less successful members of the same group. On the other hand, non-Appalachian whites of low and medium social status appear to hold negative images of Appalachians for ecological reasons: they may in fact be competing with Appalachians for employment, housing, and social services.

Stereotypes of urban Appalachians form a complex network of social status boundaries which divide along lines of race and socioeconomic status. The positive images Appalachians have of themselves are not shared by urban blacks. Negative images of Appalachians divide higher-status Appalachians from those of lower status, and separate Appalachians from working- and middle-class whites. The isolation and separation of Appalachian people living in the mountains has been largely overcome; the isolation and separation of urban Appalachians through stereotyping is still a reality.

NOTES

1. The positive labels are: loyal, religious, familistic, independent, honest, patri-
    iotic, and resourceful. The negative labels are: accent, racist, apathetic, uneduca-
    ted, alcoholic, untidy, and violent. These labels appear frequently in the literature
    on Appalachians, and are mentioned specifically as stereotypes in fifteen works
    cited by Obermiller (1982:72). Moreover, twelve of the fourteen labels overlap
    with those used by Katz and Braly (1933).

2. The statements are as follows in the order they were presented and the label they
    represent: "Appalachians seem to stand up for their friends" (loyal); "Appa-
    lachians seem to have a high regard for the Bible" (religious); "Appalachians
    often seem to be involved in violent crimes" (violent); "Appalachians seem to
    have serious drinking problems" (alcoholic); "Appalachians seem to have a strong
    concern for their families" (familistic); "Appalachians seem to get the most out of
    the resources they have" (resourceful); "Appalachians seem to be unconcerned with
    getting ahead in life" (apathetic); "Appalachians do not seem to be very neat
    about their personal property" (untidy); "Appalachians seem to be pretty self-reli-
    ant in most situations" (independent); "Appalachians do not seem to to put a very
    high value on getting an education" (uneducated); "Appalachians seem to be
    truthful in their dealings with others" (honest); "Appalachians seem to speak with
    a distinct accent" (accent); "White Appalachians seem to be unwilling to live in
    racially integrated neighborhoods" (racist). Response categories were "strongly
    agree," "agree," "disagree," "strongly disagree," "don't know," and "no answer."

3. The Appalachian Regional Commission's definition of Appalachia includes 397
    counties. The Greater Cincinnati Survey, however, deleted data on Appalachian
    migrants from Clermont County, Ohio because it is directly adjacent to Hamilton
    County, Ohio. Clermont County was excluded so that residents of eastern suburbs
    of Cincinnati who have moved into the city would not be included in the data set
    on migrants.

4. The decision to delete black Appalachians from this study was based on their
    small number (3.2% of the county's population).

5. The socioeconomic status index was created by first collapsing income, education,
    and occupation into the following categories:

Value	INCOME	EDUCATION	OCCUPATION
1	$0-14,999	Less than high school	Blue-collar
2	$15,000-24,999	High school diploma	-------------
3	$25,000 and over	Some college or more	White-collar

These three variables were then summed, resulting in an index with scores ranging from 3 to 9. Respondents with a score of 3 or 4 were classified as low SES, those with scores of 5, 6, or 7 were categorized as medium SES, and individuals with scores of 8 or 9 were categorized as high on the SES index.

6.   The score is derived according to the following formula:

$$\text{Stereotyping Score} = (Sp/Np)-(Sn/Nn)$$

where Sp is the number of positive stereotypes agreed to by a group which have a higher percentage of agreement for all groups to be compared; Np is the number of positive stereotypes; Sn is the number of negative stereotypes agreed to by a group which have a higher percentage for each stereotype than the average percentage of agreement for all groups to be compared; and Nn is the number of negative stereotypes. The stereotyping score thus derived ranges from +1 to -1, where +1 represents above-average agreement on all positive stereotypes and -1 represents above-average agreement on all negative stereotypes.

THE ETHNIC ENTREPRENEUR IN THE URBAN APPALACHIAN COMMUNITY

Sharlotte K. Neely

Estimates vary on how many urban Appalachians live in the tri-state region centering on Cincinnati, but perhaps one of the most impressive estimates is that possibly one-third of the school children in Cincinnati are Appalachian. The problem, of course, lies in defining an Appalachian. Appalachians are largely, but not exclusively, white, English-speaking, Protestant, and native-born, "just like average Americans." An academic debate has been conducted for some time about whether Appalachian subcultural differences really exist, and there are numerous publications describing the unique structure of the Appalachian family and other distinctive traits. On the other side of the argument, most recently, is historian Henry Shapiro's (1978) book, *Appalachia On Our Mind,* which suggests that the Appalachian region and people are a creation of intellectuals and have no basis in cultural reality.

In anthropology, Fredrick Barth (1969) offers a solution to the above extremes which for our purposes here may come closest to reality. In *Ethnic Groups and Boundaries,* Barth (1969:13) suggests that the "critical feature" in defining the parameters of an ethnic group are "self-ascription and ascription by others," a phenomenon which certainly exists among Cincinnati's Appalachians. As Barth (1969:13-14) explains:

A categorical ascription is an ethnic ascription when it classifies a person in terms of his basic, most general identity, presumptively determined by his origin and background. To the extent that actors use ethnic identities to categorize themselves and others for purposes of interaction, they form ethnic groups in this organizational sense.

As Barth (1969:15) goes on to elaborate, "the critical focus. . .becomes the ethnic *boundary* that defines the group, not the cultural stuff that it encloses."

Cultural signals mark the boundaries and some signals are more representative of substantial cultural differences than others. Signals based on differences in language or religion may be more significant than those based on different craft items or music.

Despite the surface evidence that Appalachians are "just like other Americans," numerous cultural signals mark off the boundaries of their ethnic identity. Appalachians certainly are English-speakers, but most speak a dialect of English which results in their ascription as Appalachians every time they open their mouths to talk. Often the ascription is the negative equivalent of Appalachian, such as "hillbilly" or "ridge-runner" or the like. Appalachians are certainly predominantly white, but in the inner cities, where significant black populations exist, whites, particularly poor ones, do stand out. Since Appalachians who become better off economically can and do often leave Appalachian neighborhoods and blend into the larger white middle class, the stereotype persists that all Appalachians are poor whites. In a city like Cincinnati, to be Protestant is not to be in the majority. Most Cincinnatians are Catholic, often middle class people of either German or Irish origin. So here being Catholic is associated with economic well-being, political power, and being a "native" of the city while to be Protestant and Appalachian is to be poor, powerless, an outsider.

A most important ethnic signal for Appalachians is that of the homeland, the region back in the mountains where one still has family ties and returns for ceremonies, holidays, and vacations. Edward Spicer (1971) refers to the homeland symbol as one of the most significant signals for an ethnic group and cites its importance for peoples as diverse as American Indians and Zionist Jews. Other signals also exist in the form of bluegrass music, mountain crafts, downhome food, an annual Appalachian Festival, and a generalized notion of distinct Appalachian values which range from a strong sense of family obligations to an idea of independence which defies all authority.

It would seem that the role of an Appalachian entrepreneur is to maximize the value in ascribing ethnically as an Appalachian and to create an innovative political program based on the ideal of ethnic pluralism. Harald Eidheim (1968) has done an excellent job of analyzing the role of the ethnic innovator in the Lappish Movement in Norway, and his work and Barth's (1966) offer insights into this situation. Barth and Eidheim have focused on the limits of the role of the individual, such as the ethnic entrepreneur, in change in an attempt to find a middle ground of analysis that falls somewhere between cultural determinism and the great man theory.

Barth (1966) tends to focus on the decisions individuals make. He assumes that individuals, operating under varying constraints and incentives, play roles which allow them to make the most rational choices possible in their own best interest. As individuals engage in new social transactions allowed by these roles, relative values are revealed through real dilemmas of imminent choice. The most basic role of the ethnic entrepreneur is to create new, more satisfying roles for the members of the ethnic group to act out.

Barth (1966:17) suggests that the relevant characteristics of the ethnic entrepreneur are that he manages the undertaking, he is an innovator, and he tries to maximize the value in ethnic identification. The entrepreneur is involved in multiple transactions and initiates new activities, such as creating political and economic bridges between the ethnic group and the dominant power structure (Barth 1966:18). A successful ethnic entrepreneur can change the basic values and ethnic identity of an entire population.

Much as in the case of Lapps in Norway, Appalachians are viewed and often view themselves as backward, inferior, and maladaptive. In such a situation, the ethnic entrepreneur often offers a "package deal" which combines the promise of a positive ethnic image with the prospect of economic and political gains. In effect, the ethnic entrepreneur creates a new role where none existed before, a role wherein ethnic identity actually aids in attempts to be successful and adaptive rather than in the past when such identity insured only failure.

The Urban Appalachian Council seems to represent one successful outcome of the larger Appalachian movement in this country, and, in my analysis, part of the reason for that organization's success is to be found in its former director, Michael Maloney, and an ethnic entrepreneur.

Maloney's basic contribution lay in his leadership ability which resulted in adequate funding and staff for the organization. It is probably no accident that the two-year existence of United Appalachians of Cincinnati ended when Maloney left the city in 1970 or that remnants of that organization splintered into two new groups with different kinds of members. Maloney has always seemed to enact the role of unifier and reconciler. One of the key problems of any social movement is the threat of factionalism. Up to a point, Maloney was able to avoid the two most obvious types of factionalism, that of "real Appalachians," usually first-generation migrants with strong ties to the mountains, versus the "not-so-real Appalachians," as well as the factionalism threatening between Appalachian people from Appalachian communities versus non-Appalachian professionals working in both research and applied roles in those communities.

The first type of factionalism, reasoned Maloney, could only surface if there were no adequate definition of who was Appalachian. So the organization defined an Appalachian operationally in three ways, as anyone who was born in the region or whose ancestors were, as anyone who shares the Appalachian folk culture, or as anyone who is intensely involved with Appalachians at the neighborhood level. The last category made the definition quite broad and could hypothetically include people not of Appalachian origin but to whom the Appalachian folk culture had diffused. It was not until 1978 that this view of an Appalachian was challenged and unsuccessfully so. Maloney himself easily falls into a "real Appalachian" ascription: born in a log cabin in eastern Kentucky, the son of a coal miner and steel worker, a migrant to Cincinnati as a young adult. His own total legitimacy as an Appalachian has probably helped Maloney in successfully expanding the definition and role of an Appalachian, since doing so is not viewed as self-serving.

The second type of factionalism, that of insiders _vs._ outside professionals, was taken care of in a different way. The Appalachian movement generally probably has its origin in organizations of non-Appalachian professionals who worked in Appalachian communities. Those people still wanted input in an Appalachian organization, and when Maloney had left the city in 1970, they had largely split off into a separate organization, the Appalachian Committee, as distinct from Appalachians like Ernie Mynatt who worked with groups like the

Appalachian Identity Center. When the Urban Appalachian Council was formed in 1974, the problem of outsiders was met in a straightforward way via the idea of advocacy which deliberately constructed a role for such people, which allowed them input, but also limited their roles in favor of Appalachians. Advocacy was defined as people who are "not a grass roots group and cannot speak for Appalachians, rather [these] members are to use their knowledge and other resources in such a way that the needs and problems of mountain migrants are documented and solutions are effected." The group also espoused the goal of promoting "efforts to organize Appalachians and to establish an organization whose sole aim is to organize in Appalachian neighborhoods." Like the other type of factionalism, this kind seems to have been avoided until 1978 when the issue was unsuccessfully challenged.

Perhaps even a third type of factionalism was avoided when Maloney consciously built in two different political ideologies into the organization in order to make room for different kinds of people. Maloney has characterized the two as "standard liberal opportunity theory" and "more radical social movement theory." Both ideologies have managed to survive, and the organization has members and staff from every political party, as well as the apolitical.

In short, Maloney meets Barth's criteria as manager of the whole operation by providing the leadership which has consistently secured funding and staff to do work on behalf of Appalachians. He meets Barth's criteria as an innovator by building bridges between the Appalachian community and the political power structure. He maintains recognition for Appalachians as an ethnic group, and that recognition manifests itself in the local media who consistently use the term Appalachian in referring to certain neighborhoods or organizations. Finally, he has maximized the value in Appalachian identity by developing a broad definition of Appalachian and convincing both Appalachians themselves and non-Appalachians of the positive contribution of the Appalachian lifestyle.

Maloney's success in Cincinnati seems all the more significant when contrasted with the failure or limited success of Appalachian organizations in other cities. The organization in Cleveland, for example, ultimately ran aground on a problem solved in Cincinnati, that of what is an Appalachian and what to do with the non-Appalachians residing in Appalachian neighborhoods. In Columbus, Ohio the insider/outsider question, as well as the problem of what an Appalachian is, doomed the group. In Chicago, and Detroit as well, there was the problem of the existence among poor whites of at least as many southerners generally as Appalachians specifically. Efforts to organize Chicago people under the negative "poor whites" label have had only sporadic success. In Dayton, Ohio there is an Appalachian organization, but being organized largely by people with a middle class orientation, it has remained largely cultural and fraternal and has not sought the funding to develop economic programs in poor Appalachian neighborhoods as Cincinnati has. Other cities with Appalachian populations have no viable Appalachian organization such as Pittsburgh, Baltimore, Washington, DC, and Atlanta.

In some towns where no Appalachian or other ethnic organizations have been founded, other groups have moved in to fill the void. The most notorious is probably the Ku Klux Klan, experiencing a national revival, which pits poor whites, whether Appalachian or otherwise, against other ethnic groups in an attempt to improve economic and political conditions. An organization like the Urban Appalachian Council addresses the legitimate grievances of its constituents, instead, to the power structure in familiar ethnic terms.

The success of the Urban Appalachian Council in organizing Appalachians ethnically for political and economic improvement is to a great degree the result of the efforts of an ethnic entrepreneur. His insights into ethnic movements have allowed the organization to avoid the factionalism and problems unsuccessfully dealt with by other groups and have laid the groundwork for a positive image of Appalachian people. The by-products of his efforts have resulted in reduced racial and ethnic tension and the improvement of people's lives.

PART TWO

Continuing Development Among Appalachian Migrants

Having established the problems prevalent among Appalachian migrants, it was necessary to know the number of people living outside the region. Clyde McCoy and James Brown (1981) first did this important work and documented their findings in *The Invisible Minority*. For a twenty-five year period commencing with the end of World War II, large numbers of Appalachians left the region. Few people moved there. However, the seventies saw a reverse pattern of migration and the eighty census revealed that Appalachia had become a receiving area for migrants from other places. While debates continue over whether Appalachia gains more people than it loses, the two papers in this section look at those people who are leaving the region. The paper by Obermiller and Oldendick provides documentation of the extent of recent outmigration and the destinations of these people. The paper by Philliber is concerned with the characteristics of these people. The changing destinations and composition of these migrants have important implications.

MOVING ON

Recent Patterns of Appalachian Migration

Phillip J. Obermiller & Robert W. Oldendick

Although migration studies make an important and useful contribution to our understanding of the Appalachian experience, patterns of recent Appalachian migration have been neglected. No effort has been made to compare current Appalachian migration patterns with previously collected data on earlier Appalachian migration patterns, nor have recent Appalachian migration flows been compared with national migration trends. In this paper we will attempt to update the study of Appalachian migration.

We will begin by examining the principal studies of Appalachian migration, and will describe the data set used in the current study. Next we will present an overview of Appalachian migration for the period 1980-81, including a brief analysis of migration flows at the state level. This discussion will be followed by a description of current migration streams to selected urban areas, along with the changes in migration to these areas that occurred between the late 1960's and the early 1980's. We will summarize these findings with a survey of recent patterns of net Appalachian migration by national regions, census divisions, states, and selected urban areas. In conclusion, we will discuss these findings both in light of the changes and continuity in Appalachian migration patterns over time and in terms of the relationship between these patterns and national migration trends.

Previous Studies

The field of regional studies has identified two basic economic options that affect migration: the distribution of economic opportunities to regional populations primarily through the creation of jobs, which inhibits migration, or the distribution of regional populations to external areas of economic opportunity, which encourages migration (Cumberland, 1973). Carter Goodrich and his associates (1936) recommended the latter option as a result of a study they made in the mid-

1930's, which included eighty-four coal-producing counties in the Cumberland Plateau. The study advocated that the number of farmers and miners in this area be reduced through the outmigration of more than a quarter of the area's population.

Brown and Hillery (1962) documented the fact that many persons did, in fact, leave the Southern Appalachian region during the twenty-year period between 1940 and 1960. Although a great deal of movement took place within the region, southern Appalachia also experienced a net loss of over thirteen percent of its population between 1940 and 1950, and a net loss of nineteen percent between 1950 and 1960 (Brown and Hillery, 1962:59). In his review of the 1970 census data, James S. Brown (1972) notes that between 1960 and 1970, outmigration from southern Appalachia continued at a considerably lower rate resulting in a net loss by migration of five percent for the decade (Brown, 1972:138). During the 1960's the metropolitan areas within southern Appalachia increased by nearly eight percent, principally through inmigration, since natural increase had declined significantly during this period, with the exception of those in Georgia, the nonmetropolitan counties in each of the ten states with Appalachian areas experienced an overall loss due to net migration (Brown, 1972:135-138).

Paralleling national trends in rural-to-urban migration, the majority of Appalachian migrants moved to large, industrialized metropolitan areas. Clyde B. McCoy and James S. Brown (1981) have documented in some detail the migration stream systems from southern Appalachia into major metropolitan areas of the country. Their study identifies the thirty top-ranking metropolitan destinations for southern Appalachian migrants, as well as the particular migration stream systems between West Virginia and Kentucky and the ten metropolitan focal areas for these systems (McCoy and Brown, 1981). Although the rate of outmigration decreased over the thirty-year period ending in 1970, McCoy and Brown find a great deal of consistency in the direction and proportions of Appalachian migration to the metropolitan focal areas they have identified.

The major finding of the Appalachian Regional Commission's Report to Congress on Migration (1979) is the turnaround in net Appalachian migration. An analysis of the Social Security Administration's continuous work history sample for 1965, 1970, and 1975 indicates that Appalachian migration changed from a net loss to the region in the period 1955-1970 to a net gain in the period 1970-75. The pattern of outmigration also changed: while Northern states remained the destination of the greatest number of Appalachian migrants, states in the South showed the largest gain in the percentage of Appalachian migrants received (Appalachian Regional Commission, 1979b: Tables 11-3 and 11-4). The report concludes that most outmigrants enjoy greater incomes than they experienced while in Appalachia, and quickly gain income parity with workers in the areas where they settle (Appalachian Regional Commission, 1979b:15).

The Current Study

The data for this study were compiled by the Bureau of the Census for the Internal Revenue Service (IRS) from the Individual Master File, which includes a record of every individual income tax return form 1040 and 1040A for 1980 and 1981. The Area-to-Area Migration Flow Data were developed by matching the social security numbers (SSNs) on returns filed in each year. When identical social security numbers were found, the counties of residence on each return were compared to see whether they matched. A match in county of residence was counted as an instance of a nonmigrant; when the counties did not match, the taxpayer was considered an outmigrant from the county of residence in the base year, and an inmigrant to the county of residence in the subsequent year. The final step in the process was to tally the exemptions on all subsequent year forms which had identical SSNs with the base year, and to categorize them as either nonmigrant, inmigrant, or outmigrant.[1]

The figures derived from the IRS Area-to-Area Migration Flow Data have several limitations which should be noted so that the data presented here may be evaluated properly. Individuals who fail to file tax returns, those who are not required to file returns, and those who inflate the number of exemptions on their returns all detract from the representativeness of the data. In addition, the IRS has applied rules to make it manageable and to protect the anonymity of individual taxpayers.[2] These characteristics of the data set make it impossible to calculate the exact volumes of migration or to describe the social characteristics of the migrants.

The definition of the Appalachian region and the definitions of metropolitan, urban, and rural counties within the Appalachian region employed in this study follow those used by the Appalachian Regional Commission (Appalachian Regional Commission, 1979a).[3] The "urban areas" referred to throughout the study are actually the counties in which the cities named are located; these areas are not necessarily congruent with the commonly used designations of urban places, urbanized areas, or metropolitan statistical areas (Weller and Bouvier, 1981). In addition, the data present migration flows for one year only; estimates for more extensive periods cannot be extrapolated accurately from this small base.

The Findings

In the twelve months covered by this study, slightly more individuals left the Appalachian region than entered it. Table 7:1 shows that the leading sources of outmigrants were the metropolitan counties in Appalachia. These counties, which had 49% of the region's 1980 population, accounted for 55% of the outmigrants. The urban counties had 25% of the population and 24% of the outmigrants; the rural counties, which had 26% of the population, contributed 21% of the outmigrants. Similar percentage distributions were found among metropolitan (54%), urban (23%), and rural (23%) Appalachian counties for the flow of migrants into the region.

Internal migration flows within Appalachia indicate that rural counties are the most frequent destinations for those who leave rural counties; of all rural-county outmigrants, 44% moved to other rural counties, 32% to urban counties, and 24% to metropolitan counties. Similarly, metropolitan counties are the most popular destination for those who leave metropolitan counties. Of all metropolitan county outmigrants, 67% moved to other metropolitan counties, 20% to urban counties, and 13% to rural counties. Residents of urban counties, however, tend to move to either rural or metropolitan counties, with a preference for the latter. In the period 1980-81, 40% of all urban county outmigrants moved to metropolitan counties, 34% to rural counties, and only 26% to other urban counties.

TABLE 7:1

1980-81 APPALACHIAN MIGRATION BY COUNTY TYPE[1]

| | Destination | | | |
Origin	Metropolitan	Urban	Rural	Out of Region
Metropolitan	119,418	35,147	22,831	289,752
Urban	34,699	22,262	29,475	127,870
Rural	22,157	30,452	41,365	114,123
Out of Region	281,845	119,830	119,671	---------

1980-81 Net Migration   -10,399

[1] For county typology see Appalachian Regional Commission, 1979.
Source: IRS Area-to-Area Migration Flow Data.

Tables 7:2a and b show the non-Appalachian states with the most significant migration flows during the period under study. When inmigrant flows are compared with outmigrant flows, it becomes apparent that reciprocal flows exist between Appalachia and California, Florida, Illinois, New Jersey, and Texas. The flows from Indiana and Michigan to Appalachia are substantially one-way streams; few migrants move to these states from the region. The flows from Appalachia to Arizona and Massachusetts are also substantially one-way, but in the opposite direction: few migrants from these states move to Appalachia.

TABLE 7:2a

MIGRATION FLOWS TO AND FROM THE APPALACHIAN REGION

Migrants to Appalachia	State	Migrants from Appalachia	State
(N)		(N)	
5,135	Florida	10,734	Florida
2,135	Illinois	10,465	Texas
2,122	New Jersey	4,849	California
1,946	California	2,207	Arizona
1,836	Michigan	1,141	Illinois
1,724	Texas	525	Massachusetts
1,266	Indiana	431	New Jersey

The non-Appalachian states that show the most significant net gains in migrants from the region are Texas, Florida, California, and Arizona, in that order. Those showing the most significant net losses are Michigan, New Jersey, Indiana, and Illinois.

Table 7:3 presents a more precise view of recent Appalachian migration. The table includes those non-Appalachian counties that had a net gain or loss of 200 or more migrants from the Appalachian region in 1980-81. Since the counties are invariably metropolitan, the name of the chief city in each county is used to designate the "urban area."

TABLE 7:2b

NET APPALACHIAN MIGRATION FOR SELECTED STATES, 1980-81.[1]

Net Gains	State
8,741	Texas
5,599	Florida
2,903	California
1,795	Arizona

Net Losses	State
-995	Illinois
-1,266	Indiana
-1,691	New Jersey
-1,784	Michigan

[1] Tables 7:2a and 2b do not include states with Appalachian counties.
Source: IRS Area-to-Area Migration Flow Data.

Houston and its environs had the largest net gain in migrants from Appalachia of any non-Appalachian urban area in the United States: it had over twice as many migrants as the second and third-ranked urban areas, Nashville and Tampa/St. Petersburg, and well above three times as many as Phoenix, Dallas, and Los Angeles, which ranked fourth, fifth, and sixth respectively.

Atlanta was the chief among those urban areas that sent more migrants to the Appalachian region than they gained, and had by far the highest combined Appalachian in- and outmigration. These facts must be interpreted with caution, however, since the county in which the city of Atlanta is located, Fulton County, shares common boundaries with five Appalachian counties. Similar conditions exist for the counties in which Cincinnati, Lexington, Roanoke, and Montgomery are located. Although these areas are likely to have high rates of exchange with neighboring counties, a situation that fulfills the technical definition of migration, their position in the ranking becomes somewhat ambiguous when compared with urban areas much more distant from Appalachia.

TABLE 7:3

SELECTED URBAN AREAS RANKED BY NET APPALACHIAN MIGRATION, 1980-81.[1]

Urban Area	Net Migration	From Appalachia	To Appalachia
Houston	6,570	7,883	1,313
Nashville	3,140	5,314	2,174
Tampa/St.Petersburg	2,992	3,684	692
Phoenix	1,635	2,047	412
Dallas	1,537	1,658	121
Los Angeles	1,482	2,851	1,369
Lexington	940	2,745	1,805
W. Palm Beach	838	1,126	288
Columbus	691	4,365	3,674
Jacksonville	623	948	325
Anaheim	593	643	50
Charlotte	576	2,033	1,457
Ft. Lauderdale	492	2,163	1,671
Mobile	401	1,162	761
Jackson	345	554	209
San Diego	320	767	447
Washington	221	331	110
Roanoke	207	860	653
Louisville	-243	300	543
Indianapolis	-258	-0-	258
Dayton	-463	395	858
Cleveland	-630	1,616	2,246
New York	-632	813	1,445
Chicago	-1,024	1,112	2,136
Miami	-1,046	644	1,690
Detroit	-1,420	52	1,472
Cincinnati	-1,933	4,366	6,299
Atlanta	-5,670	9,995	15,665

[1] Table excludes urban areas in the Appalachian region.
Source: IRS Area-to-Area Migration Flow Data.

Table 7:4 presents a comparison of the thirty top-ranked metropolitan destinations for Appalachian migrants for the periods 1965-70 and 1980-81. Nine of the destinations found in the earlier ranking–Washington, Detroit, Baltimore, Columbia, Dayton, Norfolk, Richmond, New York, and Louisville–have been replaced in the more recent rankings by Houston, Lexington, Montgomery, Ft. Lauderdale, Phoenix, Dallas, Mobile, West Palm Beach, and Jacksonville. The positions of Atlanta, Birmingham, Chattanooga, Knoxville, and Philadelphia have remained fairly constant in each order, while Chicago and Cleveland ranked significantly lower in 1981 than in the previous year. Pittsburgh, the Winston-Salem/High Point/Greensboro area, Charleston, and Greenville have all moved to substantially higher positions in the 1981 ranking.

TABLE 7:4

TOP-RANKING METROPOLITAN DESTINATIONS FOR MIGRANTS FROM SOUTHERN APPALACHIA, 1965-70,[1] AND FOR MIGRANTS FROM THE APPALACHIAN REGION, 1980-81[2]

Rank	1965-70	1980-81
1	Atlanta	Pittsburgh*
2	Washington	Atlanta
3	Detroit	Birmingham*
4	Birmingham*	Houston
5	Knoxville*	Knoxville*
6	Chicago	Chattanooga*
7	Chattanooga*	Nashville
8	Cleveland	Greenville
9	Los Angeles	Cincinnati
10	Nashville	Columbus
11	Huntington*	Tampa/St. Pete.
12	Huntsville	Charleston*
13	Baltimore	Winston-Salem/ High Point/Greensboro
14	Columbus	Huntsville*
15	Tuscaloosa*	Huntington*
16	Cincinnati	Los Angeles
17	Greenville	Lexington
18	Charlotte	Montgomery
19	Charleston*	Ft. Lauderdale
20	Columbia	Phoenix
21	Tampa	Charlotte
22	Dayton	Tuscaloosa*
23	Norfolk	Dallas
24	Richmond	Cleveland
25	New York	Mobile
26	Louisville	W. Palm Beach
27	Roanoke	Chicago
28	Winston-Salem/ High Point/Greensboro	Jacksonville
29	Pittsburgh*	Philadelphia
30	Philadelphia	Roanoke

* Located in the Appalachian region. [1] Source: McCoy and Brown, 1981.
[2] Source: IRS Area-toArea Migration Flow Data.

As elsewhere, we advise caution in examining this table because two different geographic definitions were used in constructing the rankings. In the later ranking, the *definition* of Appalachia includes counties in the states of New York, Pennsylvania, and Ohio, while the earlier definition excludes counties in these areas. This difference, for example, could be the principal reason behind the radical change in the ranking of the Pittsburgh area between one period and the other.

TABLE 7:5

NET APPALACHIAN MIGRATION TO SELECTED URBAN AREAS BY CENSUS REGIONS AND DIVISIONS, 1980-81

Census Region	Census Division	Urban Area	Net Migration	Division Totals	Region Totals
South					9,420
	South Atlantic			-2,174	
		Tampa/St. Pete., FL	2,992		
		West Palm Beach, FL	838		
		Jacksonville, FL	623		
		Charlotte, NC	576		
		Ft. Lauderdale, FL	492		
		Washington, DC	221		
		Roanoke, VA	207		
		Columbia, SC	63		
		Greensboro, NC	36		
		*Huntington, WV	19		
		Baltimore, MD	-37		
		*Charleston, WV	-434		
		Miami, FL	-1,046		
		*Greenville, SC	-1,054		
		Atlanta, GA	-5,670		
	E. South Central			3,487	
		Nashville, TN	3,140		
		Lexington, KY	940		
		Mobile, AL	402		
		Jackson, MI	345		
		*Huntsville, AL	267		
		*Knoxville, TN	256		
		*Tuscaloosa, AL	168		
		Montgomery, AL	-101		
		Louisville, KY	-243		
		*Chattanooga, TN	-503		
		*Birmingham, AL	-1,183		
	W. South Central			8,107	
		Houston, TX	6,570		
		Dallas, TX	1,537		

(Table Continued on Next Page)

Census Region	Census Division	Urban Area	Net Migration	Division Totals	Region Totals
West					4,030
	West Pacific			2,395	
		Los Angeles, CA	1,482		
		Anaheim, CA	593		
		San Diego, CA	320		
	West Mountain	Phoenix, AZ	1,635		
Northeast					-2,421
	Middle Atlantic			-2,421	
		New York, NY	-632		
		*Pittsburgh, PA	-1,789		
North Central					-5,037
	E. North Central			-5,037	
		Columbus, OH	691		
		Indianapolis, IN	-258		
		Dayton, OH	-463		
		Cleveland, OH	-630		
		Chicago, IL	-1,024		
		Detroit, MI	-1,420		
		Cincinnati, OH	-1,933		

* Indicates urban area in Appalachian region.
Source: IRS Area-to-Area Migration Flow Data.

When net migration figures for selected urban areas are categorized by census regions and regional divisions (Table 7:5), a clear pattern emerges. For 1980-81 the urban areas in the Northeast and North Central regions show losses in Appalachian migration–2,421 and 5,037 respectively–while Western states show a net gain of 4,030. Urban areas in the South have a regional net gain of 9,420 migrants from Appalachia.

At the divisional level, new losses occur in urban areas located in the South Atlantic states, despite substantial net gains in Florida, in East North Central states (5,037), and in the Middle Atlantic states (2,421). Net gains are recorded for urban areas located in the states of the East South Central (3,487), West South Central (8,107), West Pacific (2,395), and West Mountain (1,635) divisions.

Discussion

Although the evidence is incomplete, the much remarked-upon "migration runaround" of the 1970's, which saw the first net gain in migration to Appalachia in five decades, may have come to an end in the early 1980's (Picard, 1981a, 1981b). This finding would correspond to a national trend detected in the early 1980's, in which the flow of migrants to rural America decreased notably from that of the mid-1970's

(Agresta, 1985; Population Reference Bureau, 1982). Within Appalachia, however, the migrants' preference for rural counties over urban counties continued from the 1970's into the 1980's, but the flow of internal migrants away from metropolitan counties appears to have ended (Picard, 1981b). The most frequent destinations for internal migrants in this study were metropolitan counties, while the least frequent were the formerly popular urban counties.

Appalachian migrants also reflect national preferences in their choices of which states to enter and which states to leave. The 1980 census data document a preference for destinations in Texas, Florida, California, and Arizona and a disinclination to stay in Illinois, Indiana, New Jersey, and Michigan (Robey and Russell, 1983). The national migration flows to states in the South and West and away from the North and East are paralleled by the Appalachian migration patterns presented in this study (Rogerson and Plane, 1985).

In their choice of urban destinations, migrants from Appalachia go where jobs are available, but probably encounter intense competition from other migrants upon arrival. Eight of the top-ranked urban destinations of Appalachian migrants are among the twelve urban areas projected to have the greatest population growth between 1980 and 2000: Houston, San Diego, Dallas, Los Angeles, Phoenix, Anaheim, Ft. Lauderdale, and Tampa/St. Petersburg (Holdrich, 1984). Similarly, six of the top-ranked urban destinations of Appalachian migrants are among the twelve urban areas projected to have the greatest gain in employment between 1980 and 2000: Houston, Los Angeles, Anaheim, Dallas, San Diego, and Phoenix (Holdrich, 1984).

Although recent Appalachian migration patterns parallel national patterns of migration, they diverge significantly from historic patterns Appalachian migration. Brown and McCoy (1981) found high correlations among the ranking for the metropolitan destinations of Appalachian migrants in the 1950's, 1960's, and 1970's. Despite some inconsistency in the way the data were gathered for the 1965-70 study and the 1980-81 study, a substantial change in the pattern of migrant destinations in the 1980's was noted. The change is clear and consistent throughout the county, state, and regional levels of analysis. The focus of Appalachian migration has shifted from the cities and states of the Northeast and Midwest, and has now turned toward the cities and states of the South, Southwest, and West.

Conclusion

Three major conclusions can be reached on the basis of this study. First, it appears that patterns of outmigration from Appalachia changed substantially between the 1960's and 1970's and the early 1980's. The urban areas that serve as the focal points for current Appalachian migration flows are now more likely to be found in the Southern and Western states than in those of the Midwest or Northeast. Second, it appears that patterns of migration within Appalachia have changed between 1970 and 1980. Migrants within the region are moving to metropolitan counties at higher rates in the 1980's than in the previous decade. Third, outmigrants from the Appalachian region move in a fashion quite similar to other internal migrants in the United States. Current Appalachian migration streams flow toward the same general receiving areas as do the larger national migration streams. In their patterns of "moving on," recent Appalachian migrants are less similar to earlier migrants from Appalachia than to their contemporaries in other parts of the country.

NOTES

* The authors gratefully acknowledge the financial support of the Urban Appalachian Council, Cincinnati, Ohio, in obtaining the data set used in this study. The suggestions of the UAC Research and Education Committee during the data analysis stage of the study have been quiet helpful and are very much appreciated.

1. Only the returns in which the SSN in 1980 matched the SSN in 1981 were included. Reasons for nonmatches include errors in entering or reading the SSN, individuals marrying and having the second SSN on a joint return, deaths, failure to file, and falling outside the guidelines for filing.

2. When the number of returns indicating movement from one county to another were ten or less, they were aggregated into the appropriate larger category: "same state" or one of the four census regions. The present study makes no allocation of the exemptions in these categories.

    In addition, if county-to-county migration did not account for at least 0.5% of the migrants to the county of destination on the inmigration data set or at least 0.5% of the migrants from the county of origin on the outmigration data set, this information was not presented by county but included in a larger geographical category. This resulted in roughly one-third to two-fifths of the data being reported on a higher geographical level than the county-to-county level. Consequently, the figures presented in this study for county-to-county migration are quite conservative.

    Finally, since different aggregation rules may be in effect for inmigration and for outmigration data, the results produced from the two data sets are not necessarily symmetrical. An example may help to illustrate the discrepancies this may cause. In the inmigration data, where Elk County, PA, is the county of destination, the records show that 21 returns were filed by people who migrated from Allegheny County (Pittsburgh), PA. The outmigration data, in which Allegheny County is the county of origin, have no separate record for these 21 returns that indicate relocation in Elk County, but have them aggregated with other "same state" movers. These returns represent four percent of the returns for migrants into Elk County, and accordingly they are listed individually in the inmigration data; however, they account for less than 0.5% of the returns for migrants from Allegheny County, and therefore are aggregated in the "same state" category in the outmigration data. This aggregation procedure causes underestimates of the county-to-county migration into counties with large population and underestimates of the county-to-county migration out of these counties. With this in mind, we have used the outmigration data set when counties with large population were the place of destination, and the inmigration data set when these counties were the place of origin.

3. Consensus is lacking on a geographic definition of the region. In 1984 William

G. Frost defined "the Mountain Region of the South" as consisting of 194 counties (Walls, 1977); John C. Campbell (1921) included 254 counties in the "Southern Highlands"; the U.S. Department of Agriculture (1935) variously designated 205 or 236 counties as the "Southern Appalachians"; Brown and Hillery (1962) define "Southern Appalachia" as 190 counties; McCoy and Brown (1981) employ four different definitions of the region, one of which includes 303 counties; Philliber (1981) includes 396 counties in his study of Appalachian migrants and the Appalachian Regional Commission (1979a) defines the region as 397 counties. This study adopts the most inclusive definition in order to obtain the greatest range of comparability with similar research.

THE CHANGING COMPOSITION
OF APPALACHIAN MIGRANTS

William W. Philliber

The period from the end of World War II through the sixties has been described as the Great Migration out of Appalachia. During the period an estimated seven million Appalachians left, most to settle in cities surrounding the region (McCoy and Brown, 1981). A high percentage of the migrants came from low income families who brought little education with them (Philliber, 1981). They settled in neighborhoods where other Appalachians lived (Fowler, 1981; Philliber, 1981) finding work in lower blue-collar jobs (Schwarzweller, 1981).

The concentration of high numbers of people sharing a common geographic origin and similar low socioeconomic status living in the same neighborhoods created the critical mass necessary for the formation of an ethnic group. The reaction of the host communities to their presence provided the catalyst which resulted in Appalachian ethnic groups emerging in Midwestern cities (Philliber, 1981).

For the past several years a number of changes have been occurring among Appalachians living outside of the region. Taken together, these changes created reason to believe that Appalachian ethnic groups outside of the region are a temporary phenomena soon to disappear. The purpose of this paper is to examine those changes and look at their implications.

The first major change which has occurred in the pattern of Appalachian migration is that the number of people moving from Appalachia to Midwestern cities has declined. A look at the Midwestern cities included in Table 7:3 of the previous chapter shows very few migrants moving to these cities. Louisville, Indianapolis, Dayton, and Detroit all show fewer than five hundred migrants and no Midwestern city has as many as five thousand. While people may choose to debate whether net migration is to or from Appalachia, it appears that the Great Migration is over.

Not only has the Great Migration ended, it is unlikely to begin again. The population base from which migrants are drawn has declined. Fewer children are living in the region to migrate as they reach their late teens and early twenties

(*Appalachia,* 1983). The closing of coal mines and the migration from worn out farms has already taken place. Diversified manufacturing, trade, and service industries are likely to provide a more stable economic base for the region in the future. The factors which produced the Great Migration in the third quarter of this century are not present as the century ends.

The second major change in the pattern of migration out of Appalachia is a shift toward migrants who are economically better off than their predecessors. Watkins and Trevino (1982) studied women who migrated from Appalachia to Cincinnati between 1965 and 1970. They found these migrants to be disproportionately employed as professional. Again in Cincinnati, Philliber (1981) surveyed the general population in 1975 and Obermiller (1982) in 1980. If the two studies are compared, the latter study indicates that first generation white Appalachian migrants are better educated (28% compared to 15% have some college) and have better occupations (24% compared to 18% are employed as professionals or managers) than they did earlier. Although only the Watkins-Trevino study shows Appalachians doing as well as non-Appalachians, the suggestion is there that recent Appalachian migrants are economically better off than was true in earlier years.

The third major change occurring among Appalachians living outside of the region is their generation of migration. The Great Migration brought people to the Midwest in their late teens and early twenties. Many of them bore children who were second-generation Appalachians. Many of those people are now adults and have their own families–third-generation Appalachians. Both Philliber (1981) and Obermiller (1982) found as many second-generation Appalachians as they found first-generation migrants. In the conference on Appalachians held in Cincinnati in 1984, service providers in neighborhoods where Appalachians had settled described their populations as predominantly second- and third-generation Appalachians.

The history of white ethnic groups in America suggests that by the third generation ethnic ties weaken as people move into the mainstream of a community (Blau and Duncan, 1967; Goering, 1971). There are several reasons to believe this will be true of Appalachians living in Midwestern cities. A number of Appalachians remained in ports-of-entry for only a short time before they secured sufficient education to also hold middle class positions (Philliber, 1981; Obermiller, 1982). Studies cited above indicate that large numbers of current migrants are already middle class. Ethnicity is less of a factor in the lives of middle class people (Massey, 1981). For people of some economic means, socio-economic ties become stronger than ethnic ties. Middle income people have room below them. Ethnic differentiation is likely to be stronger among lower income people who have fewer human capital resources to protect them and may rely upon ethnic discrimination for security. Middle income people, less vulnerable to discrimination, lessen their ethnic ties.

Many Appalachians will not move into the middle class. Dropouts from school and unemployment remain high among children born to migrants. These second- and third-generation Appalachians will remain in decaying inner-city neighborhoods, but they are unlikely to consider themselves Appalachians or be considered so by others. First, there will be little about these people to identify them as Appalachians. The distinctive accents of their parents will be replaced by speech patterns of Midwestern city dwellers. They will have learned the ways of city people and know little of the ways people live in Appalachia. In the land of their ancestors they will be known as "city slickers" and "Yankees." Unlike the Appalachians who migrated, these people are stuck in the city. Early migrants were able to return to the mountains when employment ran out in the city. These people have no place to call home in Appalachia. Their families live outside the region. They remain poor, but they do not remain Appalachian.

New migrants from Appalachia will not replace former generations in Appalachian neighborhoods. Because they are economically better off, they will live in middle income neighborhoods. Their identification with Appalachians will be limited to collecting quilts and listening to mountain music. The economic problems suffered by previous generations and their offspring will not be their problem.

The emergence of Appalachians as an ethnic group in Midwestern cities has been an important dynamic of the third quarter of the twentieth century. However, the changes which have occurred in the last quarter will probably result in an end to Appalachian ethnicity as it existed.

PART THREE

From Regionalism To Urban Life

People of Appalachian heritage have now been a part of midwestern cities for a number of years. During that time they have affected and have been affected by that environment. Previous work documented the experiences of early migrants. This section analyzes more recent experiences. Many of the people studied in these papers were born outside of the region to parents who themselves were migrants. Others are recent migrants who moved after the period of the Great Migration. Focus is placed upon their relationship to urban forms of government, family, and education.

TWO STUDIES OF APPALACHIAN CIVIC INVOLVEMENT

Phillip J. Obermiller & Robert W. Oldendick

I. POLITICAL ACTIVITY AMONG APPALACHIAN MIGRANTS

The importance of ethnicity in the formation of a political culture among white immigrant groups has received a good deal of attention since the "ethnic renaissance" of the late 1960's and 1970's (Glazer and Moynihan, 1975). More recently, discussions and documentation of ethnic group formation among white Appalachian migrants to metropolitan areas outside the Appalachian region have begun to appear in the literature (Philliber, 1981).

Marger and Obermiller (1983) have put forth a theory of emergent ethnicity among Appalachian migrants based on a combination of four models of ethnic group formation. The first model posits the development of a culturally based community within the group in question; the second model requires the development of an ethnic identity among group members and recognition of the group by outsiders; the third depends on the development of clear ecological patterns (e.g., neighborhood or occupational clustering) which contribute to in-group solidarity; the fourth represents political mobilization of group members in response to competition from other ethnic groups.

Data relating to the first three models have been collected and analyzed. Philliber (1981) found little evidence that Appalachian migrants possess unique cultural traits. Obermiller (1982) pointed to definite patterns in the stereotyping of urban Appalachians by Appalachians as well as non-Appalachians. Other investigators (Fowler, 1981; Schwarzweller, 1981) have documented the presence of predominantly Appalachian neighborhoods in urban areas and the occupational clustering of Appalachian workers. The purpose of this article is to examine Appalachian political behavior in Hamilton County, Ohio, specifically to determine the degree to which a distinct set of political activities characterizes the county's white Appalachian population.[1]

Although a variety of historical and contemporary studies have focused on politics in the Appalachian region (Gaventa, 1980; Ryan, 1975), few have dealt with the political activities of out-migrants from Appalachia. Early studies (Giffin, 1962; Schwarzweller, Brown and Mangalam, 1971) of the political differences between Appalachian migrants and urban natives show little difference between these two groups, while later investigations (Philliber, 1981) demonstrate strong differences between them, but provide little evidence as to the reason for such distinctions. The present study first examines the factors of political involvement and affiliation in order to test which of these conflicting interpretations is more accurate, and then determines the salience of ethnicity in the political behavior of Appalachian migrants.

Analysis

The data employed in this study were collected as part of the Fall, 1980 Greater Cincinnati Study.[2] In this survey interviews were conducted with 753 white non-Appalachians, 237 white Appalachians, and 127 black non-Appalachians. Thirty-six black Applachians have been excluded from the sample because of their small number and because of a reluctance to confuse race with ethnicity in the present study (cf. Philliber and Obermiller, 1982). Respondents were coded as Appalachian if they were born in Appalachia or if at least one of their parents was born in Appalachia.[3]

Before discussing how Appalachians differ from or resemble other urban groups political activity, it is necessary to compare their position vis-a-vis these groups in terms of basic social characteristics. Appalachians in greater Cincinnati have the same general age profile and sex distribution as other whites and blacks. All three groups have lived in the area approximately the same number of years, on the average. Distinct differences appear, however, when the three groups are compared for educational attainment, occupational status, and income.

Disproportionately few Appalachians (36%) and blacks (31%) have had any college experience when compared with the non-Appalachian white population (48%). These three groups are also quite distinct in occupational status. Blacks are found disproportionately in the operative and labor/service job categories, and are underrepresented in the professional and managerial occupations when compared with both Appalachians and non-Appalachian whites. Appalachian whites differ from their non-Appalachian counterparts primarily in the high percentage of operatives in this group (19% vs. 7%) and the relatively low percentage having jobs in the sales/clerical job categories (38% vs. 26%. The distribution of family income for Appalachians and other whites in Hamilton County is quite similar, but a much higher percentage of blacks is found in the low-income range, with 46% of black families having incomes of less than $15,000.

In overall socioeconomic status, white Appalachians are distinct from both non-Appalachians and blacks.[4] White non-Appalachians are generally in the higher-status group, while a higher percentage of blacks is found in the low socioeconomic category. Appalachian whites fall between these two groups in overall socioeconomic status.

These data show some similarities among the three groups in demographic characteristics, but greater distinctions appear in social status. Is this variation among the groups also evident in their political activity? Prior research (Hill and Luttbeg, 1980; Milbrath and Goel, 1977) has shown that social-position factors such as education, occupation, and income have a significant effect on an individual's political behavior. To determine how Appalachian origin contributes to such activity, we examined two aspects of political activity, involvement and affiliation. Involvement was measured by questions on the respondents' general interest in politics, their interest in political campaigns, whether or not they voted, and whether they knew the names of their U.S. senators. The two questions which probed affiliation were related to party identification and liberal-conservative self-placement.[5]

Although the figures in Table 9:1 show variation across groups, they do not present a uniform picture concerning the involvement of each of the three groups. In general interest in politics, for example, white Appalachians and blacks are quite similar, while non-Appalachian whites are more likely to say they follow politics some of the time and are less likely to follow them "only now and then." A similar distribution occurs on the campaign interest question. Again, white Appalachians and blacks are very much alike, while white non-Appalachians are more inclined to follow politics "somewhat" and less likely to say "not much." On the question of voting, however, a lower percentage of Appalachians claims to have voted than either of the non-Appalachian groups. Regarding the question of knowing their senators' names, blacks are distinct; a much higher percentage in this group are unable to name either senator than in either of the other two groups.

Turning to the question of political affiliation, the data demonstrate differences among the three groups in regard to political identification. The figures for partisanship show blacks to be much more Democratic and much less Republican than Appalachian and other whites. On the question of self-identified political philosophy, white non-Appalachians are less likely to be liberal than either Appalachians or blacks, while a smaller percentage of blacks considers themselves conservative.

Although the variation among groups on these questions is not totally consistent, a general pattern emerges to show that white Appalachians are similar to blacks in terms of their political involvement, and that these two groups are distinct from white non-Appalachians. This description, however, leaves unanswered the question of how much Appalachian origin, as opposed to other social characteristics, contributes to these differences. To examine this question, political activity measures for involvement and affiliation were used as dependent variables in a series of multiple regressions which included income, education, race, age, sex, and Appalachian origin as independent variables.[6] In this way the effects of Appalachian origin can be specified separately from the effects of other social characteristics.

The data presented in Table 9:2 demonstrate clearly the importance of demographic factors over Appalachian origin in explaining these political variables. Education and age are the best predictors of political involvement; sex and income also contribute to the explanation of variance on this scale. Race is the best predictor of party identification, while income and age also contribute to this model. For political philosophy, age is the most important predictor variable; race and income somewhat less important. Appalachian origin contributes little to the explanation of any of these variables, and does not make a statistically significant difference for any of the dependent variables explained. While Appalachians may differ from non-Appalachian whites and blacks in various aspects of their political activity, Appalachian origin

TABLE 9:1

RESPONSES OF WHITE NON-APPALACHIANS, WHITE APPALACHIANS, AND BLACK NON-APPALACHAINS IN HAMILTON COUNTY, OHIO TO QUESTIONS REGARDING THEIR POLITICAL INTEREST, PARTICIPATION, KNOWLEDGE, AND AFFILIATION

	White non-Appalachians	White Appalachians	Black non-Appalachians
Political interest?[a]			
Most of the time	34%	39%	36%
Some of the time	37%	27%	26%
Only now and then	28%	33%	38%
N	723	225	127
Campaign interest?[a,b]			
Very much	39%	41%	45%
Somewhat	45%	33%	31%
Not much	16%	26%	24%
N	721	225	127
Voted in last election?[a,b]			
Yes	73%	61%	69%
No	27%	39%	31%
	723	227	125
Able to name senators?[a,c]			
Both	35%	31%	17%
One	29%	27%	25%
Neither	36%	43%	58%
N	726	225	127
Party identification[a,c]			
Democrat	23%	21%	56%
Independent	46%	42%	36%
Republican	32%	37%	8%
N	701	225	127
Political philosophy[a]			
Liberal	18%	25%	32%
Moderate	44%	35%	41%
Conservative	38%	39%	27%
N	681	208	108

[a]Indicates statistically significant differences at the .01 level between white non-Appalachians, white Appalachians, and black non-Appalachians using a chi-square test.

[b]Indicates statistically significant differences at the .01 level between white non-Appalachians and white Appalachians using a chi-square test.

[c]Indicates statistically significant differences at the .01 level between white Appalachians and black non-Appalachians using a chi-square test.

contributes little to the explanation of these differences when other social factors are controlled in a multivariate model.

TABLE 9:2

BETA WEIGHTS FOR REGRESSIONS ON POLITICAL
INVOLVEMENT AND AFFILIATION

	Involvement	Affiliation	
	Political Involvement	Party Identification	Political Philosophy
Education	−.38*	−.02*	−.02
Age	−.32*	.09*	.24*
Sex	.13*	−.03	.03
Income	−.11*	.13*	.09*
Race	.02	.26*	.11*
Appalachian origin	.01	−.03	.04
Multiple R	.50	.32	.28

*Statistically significant at the .01 level.

II. APPALACHIAN PARTICIPATION IN URBAN NEIGHBORHOOD GOVERNANCE

At present the city of Cincinnati recognizes 48 "statistical neighborhoods," which identify the approximate neighborhood location of census tracts and are used primarily for data collection and analysis (City Planning Commission, 1980). From another perspective, there are 47 neighborhoods with at least one "semi-official" community council operating in each. In some neighborhoods more than one council exists because of political rivalries, because they are subdivided into block clubs, or because of special-interest groups within the same neighborhood (Bordwell, 1983a). In mid-1983 there was a total of 78 neighborhood-based councils or groups and two citywide coalitions of neighborhood groups (Bordwell, 1983a, 1983b).

The Data

In the spring of 1981 the Behavioral Sciences Laboratory of the University of Cincinnati conducted the Citizens Services Survey/1981,[7] a random-digit-dialing telephone survey of 4,275 adults living in Cincinnati. The survey identified 1,185 black respondents, 325 first-generation white Appalachians, and 2,492 other whites. The research design recognized the importance of distinguishing among these three groups because of their high-density concentrations in particular Cincinnati neighborhoods (Maloney, 1974), and because they display distinct socioeconomic and ethnic characteristics (Philliber, 1981).

Two limitations inherent in this data set should be taken into consideration when reviewing the results of the study. First, the data understate the number of Appalachians by at least half by including black Appalachians in the black group and by including second-generation white Appalachians among "other whites." Second, the data were collected primarily for descriptive rather than explanatory purposes; thus the secondary analysis of such data is quite limited in its explanatory power. Even with these constraints, however, the data set is the most current and complete source of information on Appalachian participation in urban neighborhood governance.

The Results

In 1978 the Institute of Governmental Research reported that "while 71% (of Cincinnatians surveyed) know of the existence of community councils in their neighborhoods, only 12.4% report that they belong to the council" (Institute of Governmental Research, 1978:3). Five years later slightly less than 55% of Cincinnatians surveyed knew of such councils operating in their neighborhoods, and only 14% indicated that they were members of a neighborhood council. More blacks (62%) than Appalachians (44%) or other whites (53%) knew of a local neighborhood association or community council, but among those who knew of such organizations only 24% of the Appalachians and other whites and 27% of the blacks said that they belonged in some way to a neighborhood council.

TABLE 9:3

AGE AND SEX OF MEMBERS OF THREE CINCINNATI GROUPS
WHO KNOW ABOUT AND BELONG TO NEIGHBORHOOD COUNCILS

	AGE	KNOW % (N)	BELONG % (N)
BLACK	18-29 years	61 (271)	13 (35)
	30-64 years	69 (378)	35 (130)
	65 and older	53 (82)	40 (33)
APPALACHIAN	18-29 years	44 (30)	10 (3)
	30-64 years	43 (81)	31 (25)
	65 and older	45 (31)	21 (6)
OTHER WHITE	18-29 years	44 (463)	11 (48)
	30-64 years	62 (684)	30 (204)
	65 and older	47 (174)	31 (53)
	SEX	KNOW	BELONG
BLACK	Males	63 (270)	24 (65)
	Females	62 (467)	29 (134)
APPALACHIAN	Males	42 (52)	28 (15)
	Females	45 (90)	22 (20)
OTHER WHITE	Males	55 (591)	22 (128)
	Females	51 (721)	26 (183)

As Table 9:3 indicates, age makes little difference in whether Appalachians know about neighborhood councils, but among blacks and other whites, those between the ages of 30 and 64 are more likely to know about the councils. For each of the three groups, being over thirty years old increases the likelihood of belonging to a neighborhood council. In all three groups the sex of the respondents seem to have little bearing on knowledge of local councils. Sex also makes little difference in membership patterns, although Appalachian men are slightly more likely to be members than Appalachian women, in contrast to the prevalence of female council members in the other two groups.

When the figures are studied from the viewpoint of key social characteristics such as education, occupation, and income, a consistent pattern emerges. As the level of education rises for members of each group, so does the possibility that they will be aware of their community council. Having more than twelve years of education is the largest positive influence on the membership patterns of each of the three groups. Among the Appalachians in particular, an increase in educational attainment accompanies a major increase in both awareness and membership.

White-collar workers in each of the three groups are more likely than blue-collar workers to know about neighborhood councils and are more likely to belong to them. The effect of higher occupation status upon knowledge is greater for Appalachians then for blacks and whites; among Appalachians white-collar workers have significantly greater knowledge of local councils than do blue-collar workers. The effect of occupational status on membership patterns, however, is more pronounced for blacks and for other whites; it is almost negligible for Appalachians.

Home ownership has a modest positive effect on neighborhood-council awareness among members of all three groups, and a somewhat more substantial effect on the likelihood that they will actually be members of a council.

Overall, neighborhood satisfaction has a positive correlation with knowledge of neighborhood councils for Appalachians, but a slightly negative correlation for blacks and other whites. For each of the three groups and particularly among Appalachians, those who are satisfied with their neighborhoods are more likely to belong to a neighborhood council.

Conclusions

It seems, therefore, that Appalachian ethnicity has very little direct influence on the political activity of the county's Appalachian population. On the other hand, socioeconomic factors such as education, age, sex, race, and income help account for the observed differences in political involvement and affiliation found among the county residents sampled. Taken in themselves, these factors would appear to lend more credence to a social class explanation of the political differences observed than to an explanation based on ethnicity.

This is certainly the case of Appalachian knowledge of and participation in neighborhood councils. As socioeconomic status rises, a clear pattern of increasing knowledge and membership emerges for all three groups. Education and income have the strongest effect on awareness of neighborhood councils, while income has a substantial influence on council membership. In addition, homeowners who are also voters are consistently more likely to know about their neighborhood councils and to

TABLE 9:4

EDUCATIONAL ATTAINMENT, OCCUPATIONAL STATUS, INCOME,
AND SOCIOECONOMIC STATUS (SES) FOR MEMBERS OF THREE
CINCINNATI GROUPS WHO KNOW ABOUT AND BELONG TO
NEIGHBORHOOD COUNCILS

			KNOW % (N)	BELONG % (N)
EDUCATION	BLACK	Less than 12 yrs.	55 (217)	29 (63)
		12 years	61 (266)	19 (50)
		More than 12 yrs.	72 (253)	34 (87)
	APPALACHIAN	Less than 12 yrs.	27 (32)	9 (3)
		12 years	46 (49)	21 (10)
		More than 12 yrs.	63 (61)	35 (21)
	OTHER WHITES	Less than 12 yrs.	39 (189)	18 (33)
		12 years	49 (382)	18 (66)
		More than 12 yrs.	61 (741)	29 (211)
OCCUPATION	BLACK	White Collar	67 (264)	35 (94)
		Blue Collar	61 (410)	24 (96)
	APPALACHIAN	White Collar	59 (81)	26 (21)
		Blue Collar	34 (52)	22 (11)
	OTHER WHITES	White Collar	59 (882)	27 (239)
		Blue Collar	46 (355)	17 (60)
INCOME	BLACK	Less than $15,000	61 (318)	24 (75)
		$15,000-$30,000	71 (195)	28 (54)
		More than $30,000	76 (73)	53 (38)
	APPALACHIAN	Less than $15,000	36 (47)	16 (8)
		$15,000-$30,000	60 (54)	17 (9)
		More than $30,000	57 (22)	60 (13)
	OTHER WHITES	Less than $15,000	43 (341)	16 (53)
		$15,000-$30,000	55 (421)	22 (91)
		More than $30,000	70 (291)	32 (93)
SES	BLACK	High	74 (108)	46 (50)
		Medium	70 (237)	26 (64)
		Low	59 (199)	24 (47)
	APPALACHIAN	High	69 (36)	46 (16)
		Medium	50 (58)	14 (8)
		Low	33 (25)	12 (3)
	OTHER WHITES	High	69 (420)	32 (133)
		Medium	50 (463)	18 (83)
		Low	41 (125)	14 (17)

belong to them than renters who do not vote. Except for Appalachians, people who are dissatisfied with their neighborhoods are likely to be less aware of local councils and almost totally uninvolved in them.

The larger the income, the greater the possibility that members of all three groups will know about and be members of neighborhood councils. Among non-Appalachian whites, increasing income makes it most likely that they will know about their local councils; by contrast, Appalachian council membership increases most substantially as income rises.

One method of summarizing the combined effects of educational attainment, occupational status, and income is to combine them in such a way as to indicate the relationship of socioeconomic status (SES) within each group to awareness of neighborhood councils and membership in the councils.[8] Overall, the higher the level of socioeconomic well-being, the greater the probability of knowing about and belonging to a neighborhood council. In fact, rising socioeconomic status appears to

TABLE 9:5

POLITICAL PARTICIPATION, HOME OWNERSHIP, AND NEIGHBORHOOD
SATISFACTION OF MEMBERS OF THREE CINCINNATI GROUPS WHO
KNOW ABOUT AND BELONG TO NEIGHBORHOOD COUNCILS

			KNOW % (N)	BELONG % (N)
POLITICAL PARTICIPATION	BLACK	Voters	69 (408)	40 (161)
		Nonvoters	56 (328)	12 (38)
	APPALACHIAN	Voters	59 (88)	31 (27)
		Nonvoters	31 (54)	13 (7)
	OTHER WHITES	Voters	65 (860)	30 (252)
		Nonvoters	39 (451)	13 (59)
HOME OWNERSHIP	BLACK	Owners	69 (296)	40 (116)
		Rent	59 (440)	19 (83)
	APPALACHIAN	Owners	45 (80)	33 (26)
		Rent	44 (62)	13 (8)
	OTHER WHITES	Owners	65 (838)	30 (252)
		Rent	41 (461)	12 (56)
NEIGHBORHOOD SATISFACTION	BLACK	Satisfied	62 (575)	28 (158)
		Dissatisfied	64 (129)	22 (29)
	APPALACHIAN	Satisfied	47 (130)	27 (34)
		Dissatisfied	26 (10)	0 (0)
	OTHER WHITES	Satisfied	53 (1147)	24 (276)
		Dissatisfied	54 (128)	21 (26)

have the greatest effect among Appalachians: high-SES Appalachians are more than twice as likely to know about community councils and almost four times as likely to belong to a community council than their low-SES counterparts.

Apart from basic social characteristics, we can expect other factors to affect community council awareness and membership. Political participation, home ownership, and overall neighborhood satisfaction can be related to the knowledge of neighborhood councils and the motivation to join them. Respondents who indicated that they voted in the last Cincinnati city council election were more likely to know about their neighborhood councils and to belong to them than those who did not vote. The effect of political participation on neighborhood council membership patterns is most evident among blacks, who were over three times more likely to belong to a council if they were voters than if they were nonvoters.

Cincinnati's black residents are consistently more likely to know about and to join neighborhood-based organizations than are Appalachians or other whites. The relatively high levels of black awareness and participation in Cincinnati's neighborhood-based organizations resemble national patterns of black participation in voluntary organizations (Antunes and Gaitz, 1975; Cohen and Kapsis, 1978; Williams, et al., 1973, 1977). On the other hand, awareness and membership are lowest among the Appalachians surveyed; within the Appalachian group those with less income, less schooling, and lower occupational status are least likely to know of or be members of neighborhood councils.

Other issues in this area remain to be explored, such as the effect of community organizers on Appalachian membership in local councils and different patterns of community-council participation in heavily Appalachian neighborhoods. Nonetheless, these basic insights can be derived from this consideration of the social factors influencing neighborhood council awareness and participation among Appalachians. First, because urban Appalachians are consistently more aware of their local councils than they are willing to join them, the councils may benefit from reevaluating the wisdom of depending on public announcements (e.g., newspaper coverage, circulars, posters) to bring in Appalachian members. Second, because those groups with greater ethnic self-awareness, such as blacks, are proportionately more involved in local councils, less self-conscious groups, such as Appalachians may need more intensive recruitment to ensure adequate representation in neighborhood council membership. Third, to the extent that among Appalachians those under thirty years of age, women, and individuals of lower socioeconomic status are less well represented in local council membership, extra effort is necessary either to recruit them to council membership or to identify and act on the issues which most concern them.

NOTES

1. Hamilton County and its largest urban center, the city of Cincinnati, have long been major destinations for Appalachian migrants (McCoy and Brown, 1981). In 1980 there were over 213,000 first- and second-generation Appalachians in the county, constituting just under one-fourth of its population (Obermiller, 1982).

2. The Greater Cincinnati Survey is a cost-shared semiannual telephone survey of

residents 18 years of age and older in Hamilton County. Random-digit dialing procedures are used for selecting the sample. The response rate for this survey, including partially completed interviews, was 78.3%.

3. At the suggestion of one of the reviewers, the analysis was performed with only first-generation respondents coded as Appalachian. As would be expected, first-generation Appalachians were older and less educated than second-generation respondents, but these distinctions did not alter the relationships between Appalachian origin and other demographic characteristics, or the relationships with the political variables examined. This finding is consistent with the work of Philliber (1981) and Obermiller (1982), who have shown that generation makes little difference in the attitudes and behavior of Appalachians. Given the greater statistical power which a definition using both Appalachian generations provides, we chose this operationalization.

4. The socioeconomic status index was created by first collapsing income, education, and occupation into the following categories:

Value	Income	Education	Occupation
1	$0-$14,999	Less than high school	Blue-collar
2	$15,000-$24,999	High school diploma	
3	$25,000 and over	Some college or more	White-collar

These three variables were then summed, resulting in an index with scores ranging from 3 to 9. Respondents with a score of 3 or 4 were classified as low SES, those with scores of 5, 6, or 7 were considered medium SES, and individuals with scores of 8 or 9 were categorized as high on the SES index.

5. These questions used the same wording as those in the National Election Studies conducted by the Center of Political Studies at the University of Michigan for the variable indicating interest in politics, voting behavior, party identification, and political philosophy. Political knowledge was measured by asking respondents the following question: "Now we know that a lot of people don't always follow politics, but do you happen to know the names of the two United States senators from Ohio?"

6. The variables which have been examined here represent two dimensions of political activity: involvement and affiliation. For this regression analysis, the involvement variables—interest in politics, campaign interest, vote, and knowlede of senators' names—were combined linearly into an index which was used as one of the dependent variables. Scores on this index ranged from 4 to 12. Separate regressions were run, with party identification and political philosophy as the dependent variables. The seven-point party identification and political philosophy measures were used as dependent variables.

7. Thanks to Dean Watkins of the Office of Research, Evaluation, and Budget, City of Cincinnati, for making the Citizen Services Survey 1981 data available for this study.

8. Socioeconomic status was determined by considering level of income (less than

$15,000; $15,000-$30,000; more than $30,000), education (less than 12 years; 12 years; more than 12 years), and occupational status (white-collar; blue-collar) and combining them into appropriate categories, in this case high, medium, and low. A respondent with at least two out of three characteristics in the same category was included in that category.

10

THE IMPACT OF THE URBAN MILIEU ON THE APPALACHIAN FAMILY TYPE

James K. Crissman

Urbanization has produced a great number of changes in American society. Along with industrialization, urbanization has changed the United States from a rural society to a predominantly urban society. Especially affected have been the five major social institutions: politics, education, religion, economics, and the family.

Perhaps the institution that has been affected the most has been the family. The sociological literature indicates that the family has changed from an extended family type to a nuclear family type. Parsons (1951:510) maintains that urbanization, technology, and bureaucratization have produced an "isolated nuclear family." According to Parsons (1955a:9; 1955b:354) and Zelditch (1955:307), the modern American family, especially the urban family, is the product of the transition from an extended family type in which there is a great deal of dependence on the kinship network, to a nuclear family type in which there is a great deal of isolation from the kinship unit.

The modern nuclear family tends to occupy a separate dwelling apart from the family of orientation of either parent. The household is economically independent of the kinship unit. Parsons (1955a:9) maintains that the modern nuclear family is a product of "adaptive-upgrading" and is a more stable, improved type of family.

Leslie (1973:18, 53, and 213) suggests that urbanization and industrialization have been instrumental in producing movement toward the nuclear family as the dominant family type. Goode (1963) has proposed that, concomitant with the trend of society toward modernization, industrialization, and urbanization, the extended family becomes rare and the corporate kin structure disappears. Zimmerman (1947) and Wirth (1938) express the view that the American family is characteristically of the isolated nuclear form. Gleason (1956) maintains that the younger generation objects to joint living arrangements and it is only with reluctance that most older people will give up their freedom and become members of their children's household. McKee and

Robertson (1975:387) state that the nuclear family is the established family form in America.

FAMILY TYPE IN CENTRAL APPALACHIA. The early frontiersmen who settled in the Central Appalachian mountains (Southwestern Virginia, West Virginia, Eastern Tennessee, and Eastern Kentucky) tended to come seeking isolation. The isolation sought and secured by these settlers was conducive to the development of an extended family type. Outsiders were considered to be interested only in exploitation (Appleby, 1970:34), so the extended family and extended kinship network became important to the mountaineer.

The development of the extended family type made each valley the domain of a single family. The extended family was responsible for the specialized roles of religion, education, government, and even the military through the defense of the family (Gibson, 1975:5). These specialized roles were taken over by clans or groupings of extended families as they developed. The military role of the clan is best exemplified by such conflicts as the Hatfield-McCoy and Allen-Edwards feuds in the late 1800's and early 1900's (Caudill, 1963).

The literature indicates that the extended family is still very much in existence in Central Appalachia. Brown and Schwarzweller (1974:64) in an extensive study of the Appalachian family found that the extended family continues to be important. Some noted Appalachian scholars maintain that the extended family is still the typical family type in the Central Appalachian Mountains. Gazaway (1974:94) in her study of a Kentucky mountain community found that most family situations consisted of three generations of a family group. Stephenson (1968:2) learned that related families tend to live in at least the same neighborhood. He also discovered that it was unusual to find a family that had no kin—at least a second cousin or uncle by marriage—in other neighborhoods. One of the most noted of Appalachian authors, Weller (1966:13) states:

> It is not unusual today to find families with four generations living side by side in one narrow valley—brothers, sisters, aunts, uncles, nieces, nephews, and cousins—intermarrying to such an extent that in some fashion every person is related to every other. It frequently happens that a girl marries and does not even have to change her last name.

A major factor in the continued existence of the extended family in Central Appalachia has been endogamy. Vincent (1898), while visiting the hills of Kentucky, noted that there were isolated mountain families living up hollows and coves with strong ties of kinship based upon three or more generations of intermarriage. Matthews (1966:10) states that:

> . . . cousin marriages and the tendency for brothers and sisters to choose mates who are themselves either siblings or first cousins is evident. For siblings of one group to marry siblings of another is considered ideal and provides security in time of emergency.

Matthews (1966:xxiii) further states:

The condition intervening between kinship and other social networks is local endogamy, the practice of choosing a marriage partner within the bounds of the community. Endogamy must have had its beginning with geographical isolation and valley families' practice of marrying "conveniently" and it persists because it supposedly provides structural stability. It provides economic stability, since marrying into a neighboring farm means land and consolidates and conserves wealth. It provides cohesion insofar as marriage between persons allied by blood continually strengthens the kin network and reinforces the "mechanical solidarity" that operates in such a system, and it gives personal satisfaction inasmuch as persons marry those whom they are expected to marry and whose way of life they share.

The present study was devoted to an analysis of family type in the urban milieu. The author wanted to determine whether the urban environment is conducive to the development of a nuclear family type. To perform this task, a group of urban migrants from a rural geographical area where the extended family is still commonly found had to be studied.

While the extended family type is considered to be prevalent in Central Appalachia, the sparse studies of the family type of urban Central Appalachians have indicated that the nuclear family type is dominant. Weller (1975:110) and Schwarzweller, Brown, and Mangalam (1971:130 & 286) state that the migrants' household is typically a complete nuclear family unit composed of husband, wife, and their children. Those who do not join an established household when they move to the city usually locate in the immediate vicinity of kinfolk and friends. However, they rapidly take on the characteristics of the nuclear family. Schwarzweller, Brown, and Mangalam (1971) found that in 85.5% of the cases they studied, the household was a complete nuclear family unit; in most of the other cases (8.7%) it could be classified as an extended family unit.

Since the literature suggests the prevalence of an extended family unit in Central Appalachia and the prevalence of a nuclear family type among Central Appalachian migrants, it was felt that urban Central Appalachians would be an adequate group to study. Therefore, the family type of a group of Central Appalachian migrants was examined and then compared with the family type of non-Central Appalachian migrants in the urban milieu.

Procedure

The population in this investigation consisted of families in Akron, Ohio whose names were listed in the current *Telephone Directory for Akron and Vicinity*. The sample consisted of a random sample of 312 families residing in Akron whose names were listed in the telephone directory.

Three hundred names were initially selected, through the random selection procedure to serve as interviewees. A list of two hundred additional names was compiled (employing the same procedure used in compiling the initial list) and utilized when potential interviewees on the original list could not be reached or refused to participate.

FAMILY BACKGROUND. Respondents were classified as either Central Appalachian migrants or non-Central Appalachian migrants. Central Appalachian migrants were those who moved to the Akron, Ohio area after spending their lives in the Central Appalachian mountains. Non-Central Appalachian migrants were those persons who had lived their entire lives in Akron or had moved to Akron from somewhere outside the Central Appalachian area (these persons had never resided in Central Appalachia).

Seventy-three (23% of the total sample) of the persons participating in the study were Central Appalachian migrants. Fifty-one (73%) were from West Virginia, eight (11%) were from Eastern Kentucky, twelve (16%) were from Eastern Tennessee, and two (3%) were from Southwestern Virginia.

Two hundred thirty-nine (77% of the total sample) of the interviewees were non-Central Appalachian migrants. One hundred forty-four (46% of the total sample) were persons who had lived in Akron all their lives and ninety-five (31% of the total sample) were individuals who had moved to Akron from somewhere other than Central Appalachia.

FAMILY TYPE. Family type was classified as either nuclear or non-nuclear. Billingsley's (1968) classification of families as nuclear, extended, or augmented was originally employed. However, since only two families were classified as augmented, families determined to be extended and augmented were combined into the non-nuclear category. Twenty-two (7%) of the families were considered to be non-nuclear and two hundred ninety (93%) were classified as nuclear.

Results

The cross-tabulation of family background and family type revealed a significant difference between Central Appalachian migrants and non-Central Appalachian migrants in Akron, Ohio in relation to present family type (X^2=7.817; p< 0.01). The measure of association (C=0.17) indicates that Central Appalachian migrants are slightly more likely than non-Central Appalachian migrants to live in non-nuclear families and non-Central Appalachians are slightly more likely to live in nuclear families than Central Appalachian migrants.

While a difference is indicated, it may not be an important difference. An examination of cell frequencies and percentages (Table 10:1) indicates that there is little percentage difference between Central Appalachian migrants and non-Central Appalachians in terms of family type. Both are much more likely to reside in nuclear families than non-nuclear families. Ninety-three percent (190) of the respondents in this investigation were living in nuclear families. Eighty-five percent (62) of the Central Appalachian migrant families and ninety-five percent (228) of the non-Central Appalachian migrant families were nuclear.

Present Family Type And Family Type
Of The Family Of Orientation

Socialization is an important process in the life of an individual. Flacks (1979:23) states that the family is "the primary institution for the inculcation of basic

TABLE 10:1

CROSS-TABULATION OF FAMILY BACKGROUND AND PRESENT FAMILY TYPE

Present Family Type	Central Appalachian Migrant Frequency	%	Non-Central Appalachian Migrant Frequency	%	Total Frequency	%
Nuclear	62	85%	228	95%	290	93%
Non-Nuclear	11	15%	11	5%	22	7%
Total	73	100%	239	100%	312	100%
X^2=7.817.	df=1		p<0.01		C=0.17	

values and molding of culturally appropriate character structures. "Leslie (1969) notes that the individual develops family values and attitudes toward the family early in life.

If it is the case that family values and attitudes toward the family are developed during the early years, one would expect persons from nuclear families to establish nuclear families of procreation and persons from non-nuclear families of orientation to establish non-nuclear families.

The results of the present study indicate that persons living in nuclear families tende to come from nuclear families of orientation, but people residing in non-nuclear families also tended to come from nuclear families (Table 10:2). The vast majority of the respondents in the study lived in nuclear families of procreation and nuclear families of orientation.

CENTRAL APPALACHIAN MIGRANTS. Eighty-four percent (61) of the Central Appalachian migrants in the study lived in nuclear families of orientation. Eighty-nine percent (55) of the interviewees living in nuclear families of procreation had lived in nuclear families of orientation. Fifty-four percent (6) of those living in non-nuclear families had lived in nuclear families of orientation. These are important results in that they indicate that the majority of the Central Appalachians had lived in nuclear families prior to establishing their own family units. They also indicate (in contrast to the literature) that the majority of those families that were non-nuclear in Akron had lived in nuclear families of orientation, and that the majority of those whose family of orientation had been non-nuclear established nuclear families of procreation in the city.

OTHER MIGRANTS. Eighty-eight percent (84) of those persons who had moved to Akron from somewhere outside of Central Appalachia (other migrants) had lived in nuclear families of orientation. Eighty-nine percent (83) of those living in nuclear families had lived in nuclear families of orientation. Only one person residing in a non-nuclear family had lived in a nuclear family of orientation and one person residing in a non-nuclear family of procreation had lived in a non-nuclear family of orientation.

TABLE 10:2

CROSS-TABULATION OF FAMILY TYPE OF THE FAMILY OF
ORIENTATION AND PRESENT FAMILY TYPE

| Family Type of the Family of Orientation | Present Family Type | | | | | |
| | Nuclear | | Non-Nuclear | | Total | |
	Frequency	%	Frequency	%	Frequency	%
Nuclear	256	88%	14	64%	270	87%
Non-Nuclear	34	12%	8	36%	42	13%
Total	290	100%	22	100%	312	100%

AKRONITES. Eighty-seven percent (125) of the persons who had lived in Akron, Ohio all their lives had resided in nuclear families of orientation. Eighty-seven percent (118) of those persons presently living in nuclear families had lived in nuclear families of orientation. Seventy-eight percent (7) of those respondents living in non-nuclear families had lived in nuclear families of orientation.

Present Family Type and Family Type Directly Prior to Moving to Akron

The results of this study indicated that, by far, the majority of the respondents were living in nuclear families and had lived in nuclear families of orientation. It seemed logical to expect, on the basis of these findings, that the family type directly prior to moving to Akron, for Central Appalachian migrants and non-Central Appalachian migrants would also be nuclear. Further analysis tended to support this expectation.

Ninety-nine percent (153) of those residing in nuclear families had lived in nuclear families prior to moving to Akron. Twelve (92%) of those living in non-nuclear families had lived in nuclear families prior to moving, and only one person living in a non-nuclear family had lived in a non-nuclear family.

CENTRAL APPALACHIAN MIGRANTS. Ninety-seven percent (71) of the Central Appalachian migrants had lived in nuclear families prior to moving to Akron. Ninety-eight percent (61) of the respondents living in nuclear families had lived in nuclear families prior to moving to Akron. Ten (91%) of the Central Appalachian migrants living in non-nuclear families had lived in nuclear families.

Again, we see the pattern. Most of the Central Appalachian migrants were living in nuclear families and tended to move from nuclear family situations. Also, those residing in non-nuclear family types, in defying the literature, tended to move from nuclear family situations. Importantly, only two of the family types directly prior to moving were non-nuclear.

OTHER MIGRANTS. Ninety-nine percent (94) of the other migrants resided in nuclear families prior to moving to Akron. Ninety-nine percent (92) of those living in nuclear families had lived in nuclear families before moving. The two persons presently residing in a non-nuclear family type had resided in a nuclear family before moving.

TABLE 10:3

CROSS-TABULATION OF FAMILY TYPE DIRECTLY PRIOR
TO MOVING TO AKRON AND PRESENT FAMILY TYPE
(CENTRAL APPALACHIAN MIGRANTS AND OTHER MIGRANTS)

Family Type Directly Prior to Moving to Akron	Present Family Type					
	Nuclear Frequency	%	Non-Nuclear Frequency	%	Total Frequency	%
Nuclear	153	99%	12	92%	165	98%
Non-Nuclear	2	1%	1	8%	3	2%
Total	155	100%	13	100%	168	100%

Present Family Type And
Family Type Since Living in Akron

Based on the results previously discussed, the author decided to determine whether respondents had, during their residence in Akron, ever lived in a family type different from their present one.

Twenty percent (64) of the sample had lived in non-nuclear families at some time during their life in the city. Only fourteen percent (42) of those persons living in nuclear families had ever lived in non-nuclear family situations since residing in Akron.

TABLE 10:4

CROSS-TABULATION OF FAMILY TYPE SINCE LIVING
IN AKRON AND PRESENT FAMILY TYPE

Family Type Since Living in Akron	Present Family Type					
	Nuclear Frequency	%	Non-Nuclear Frequency	%	Total Frequency	%
Nuclear	248	86%	0	0%	248	80%
Non-Nuclear	42	14%	22	100%	64	20%
Total	290	100%	22	100%	312	100%

Twenty-six percent (19) of the Central Appalachian migrants, sixteen percent (15) of the "other migrants," and twenty-one percent (30) of the Akronites had lived in non-nuclear families at some time since living in Akron.

Conclusions

The original purpose of this study was to determine whether the urban environment is a determining factor with regard to family type. It has provided little evidence to indicate that this is the case.

The primary goal was to compare Central Appalachian migrants with non-Central Appalachian migrants because the literature suggested that the non-nuclear family was more prevalent in the Central Appalachian mountains. The results indicate that, regardless of family background, the vast majority of the respondents (1) resided in nuclear families, (2) lived in nuclear families of orientation, (3) resided in nuclear families directly prior to moving to Akron (Central Appalachian migrants and other migrants), and (4) had lived in nuclear families since living in Akron.

This investigation has provided an important indication that updated studies of present family type in Central Appalachia need to be performed. There is every indication that studies of family type in Central Appalachia are outdated and somewhat restricted in terms of geographic locale. Only after more updated studies have been performed can we draw more accurate conclusions concerning the comparison of Central Appalachian migrants and other persons in the urban milieu.

11

EFFECTS OF SCHOOLS & SCHOOLING ON APPALACHIAN CHILDREN IN CINCINNATI

Michael E. Maloney & Kathryn M. Borman

Thomas Wagner's Appalachian School Project Committee (1973) established the groundwork for study of the experience of Appalachian children in public education. Sponsored by the Urban Appalachian Council in cooperation with the Cincinnati Human Relations Commission, study group members conducted extensive observations and interviews during the spring of 1974 in three predominantly Appalachian public schools in Cincinnati: Oyler Elementary School, Roberts Junior High School, and Western Hills High School. Although interviews were carried out with teachers and administrators as well as with students, the results of interviews with students were most revealing. Students expressed a strong orientation toward neighborhood and family (as detailed, for example, in reports on relationships with siblings and frequency of family visits to kin in the mountains) and, by contrast, widespread alienation from the schools' academic and extracurricular programs.

Principally as a result of the recommendations of Wagner's committee, Cincinnati Public Schools, beginning in 1973, obtained data on county of birth for students enrolled in city schools, their parents and grandparents. These data enabled researchers to systematically determine the ethnic composition of the area schools.

Soon other studies followed. In order to establish a relationship between student dropout rates and aggregate student (i.e., school) characteristics, Marvin Berlowitz and Henry Durand (1977) isolated a set of school-related variables including student characteristics such as racial or ethnic background, self-concept and family income. In this study a school with 40% or more first, second, and third generation students of Appalachian origin was considered predominantly Appalachian. Results indicated that factors associated with high dropout rates in these schools were high rates of absenteeism (Pearson r=.68), low reading achievement (Pearson r=.89) and high rates of student suspension (Pearson r=.49). By identifying specific variables related to student alienation (dropping out), Berlowitz and Durand amplified the important finding in Wagner's study of widespread student antipathy toward school.

COMPARING THE NEIGHBORHOODS.   A   comparison   of   Cincinnati neighborhoods on adult education and youth dropout rates shows how the education problem   in   Cincinnati   is   distributed   geographically.   In   Table   11:1   the neighborhoods are listed by their 1970 socioeconomic status rank (Maloney, 1974). A look at the educational statistics show that percent of high school graduates and school dropouts   varies greatly   according   to   the   socioeconomic   status   of   the neighborhoods. Some of the higher rates are in such low SES areas as Camp Washington (49.6), Lower Price Hill (57.8), and Over-the-Rhine (44.8). High SES areas such as North Avondale (2.2) and Hyde Park (4.2) have relatively low dropout rates. The dropout problem is clearly a city wide problem, however. Even Hyde Park had twenty 16-19-year-old dropouts in 1980 and Westwood had 246.

TABLE 11:1

ADULT EDUCATION AND YOUTH DROPOUT AND JOBLESS RATES FOR CINCINNATI
NEIGHBORHOODS LISTED BY 1970 SOCIOECONOMIC STATUS RANK

CIVILIANS 16-19 YRS OLD, 1980

Socio-Economic Status Rank 1970	1980	Statistical Neighborhood	Population 1980	% Black	Percent High School Graduates (25 years or older) 1970	1980	Total no.	Not Enrolled in school %	Not High School Grad. %	Jobless (Unemployed or not Labor Force) %
1	2	Camp Washington	2,198	10.5	14.9	28.0	119	62.18	49.58	49.5
2	8	East End*	3,230	12.6	11.7	24.0	266	46.61	36.46	28.6
3	5	Lower Price Hill	2,155	0.5	15.1	23.3	161	72.05	57.76	47.2
4	4	North Fairmont-English Woods*	5,889	60.9	----	30.2	474	49.36	36.70	29.5
5	NR	Queensgate[1]	190	61.6	21.0	-----	145	80.70	66.20	51.7

Socio-Economic Status Rank 1970 1980		Statistical Neighborhood	Population 1980	% Black	Percent High School Graduates (25 years or older) 1970 1980		Total no.	Not Enrolled in school %	Not High School Grad. %	Jobless (Unemployed or not Labor Force) %
6	1	South Cummings-ville-Millvale	4,908	92.2	20.2	28.0	535	22.61	11.58	6.0
7	11.5	West End	12,886	94.8	20.5	29.0	964	25.82	17.84	13.3
8	9	Riverside-Sedams-ville	3,007	0.7	19.9	31.8	249	61.84	50.20	45.4
9	3	Over-the-Rhine	11,914	66.7	15.2	21.2	758	54.74	44.8	37.7
10	13	Walnut Hills	9,912	90.4	24.3	38.2	679	33.87	24.30	21.2
11	14	Mount Auburn	8,889	72.6	31.0	50.0	855	31.22	20.93	19.8
12	28	Fairview-Clifton Heights	7,940	10.0	27.8	53.0	457	36.10	18.16	10.7
13	11.5	South Fairmont	4,104	5.8	26.1	39.0	308	61.04	46.75	28.2
14	27	Corry-ville	4,539	52.1	38.9	60.2	236	34.32	22.88	19.1
15	25	Riverside-Sayler Park*	1,301	6.2	28.5	52.7	63	57.14	42.15	33.3
16	6	Winton Hills*	7,711	88.8	30.5	50.1	696	30.17	20.11	15.9
NR	21	Winton Place*	2,739	11.7	---	47.6	179	46.36	17.87	17.9

Socio-Economic Status Rank 1970 1980		Statistical Neighborhood	Population 1980	% Black	Graduates (25 years or older) 1970 1980		Total no.	Not Enrolled in school %	Not High School Grad. %	Jobless (unemployed or not Labor Force %
17	18.5	Carthage	2,782	0.0	24.3	40.6	147	51.07	40.13	32.7
18	15	Avondale	19,845	77.2	36.3	44.0	1,451	28.80	19.36	13.4
19	17	Evanston	9,089	92.3	30.0	46.5	832	26.20	11.29	6.5
NR	23	Evanston-E. Walnut Hills*	2,241	67.7	39.6	53.3	142	23.23	6.33	6.3
20	16	East Price Hill	20,361	4.4	33.6	43.8	1,495	49.83	32.48	19.9
21	18.5	Northside	11,884	12.4	31.6	45.6	894	48.88	32.77	21.9
22	45	Mount Adams	1,958	4.1	45.8	81.0	43	27.90	---	---
23	29	California	636	0.0	16.9	55.9	49	40.81	26.53	---
24	20	Madison-ville	12,242	55.9	42.6	53.4	853	30.94	15.59	9.1
25	30	Oakley	11,801	2.9	45.6	59.4	654	38.22	20.03	12.8
26	22	Sayler Park	3,384	1.9	44.8	58.8	288	44.79	21.87	14.2
27	36	University Heights	10,526	12.7	61.9	74.1	2,825	1.4	0.92	4.3
28	31.5	West Price Hill	20,218	0.4	45.7	60.5	1,369	29.80	14.24	6.4
29	31.5	Central Business District-Riverfront	2,528	18.8	41.8	67.3	93	48.38	6.45	6.7

Socio-Economic Status Rank 1970 1980		Statistical Neighborhood	Population 1980	% Black	Percent High School Graduates (25 years or older) 1970 1980		Total no.	Not Enrolled in school %	Not High School Grad. %	Jobless (Unemployed or not Labor Force) %
30	NR	North-West Fairmont*	---	---	36.5	---	---	---	---	---
NR	10	Fay Apartments*	3,159	91.2	---	58.6	178	29.77	20.22	12.4
31	46	Mount Look out*	3,533	.001	---	91.4	157	13.37	8.91	---
NR	39	Columbia Tusculum*	3,132	3.9	46.9	74.1	156	33.96	14.47	5.7
NR	7	Linwood*	1,425	0.3	---	30.0	111	62.16	14.46	36.9
32	42	Rose lawn^2	3,541	47.7	59.0	55.6	249	41.36	13.25	13.3
33	37	East Walnut Hills	4,106	32.9	59.6	74.1	192	19.79	13.75	3.1
34	24	Bond Hill	11,408	69.6	53.6	56.8	755	30.06	12.84	8.6
35	33.5	Hartwell	5,394	10.7	41.7	62.1	229	30.6	10.48	4.4
36.5	43	Clifton	9,240	12.3	70.7	84.1	490	22.9	16.12	12.9
36.5	26	Kennedy Heights	6,591	75.5	61.0	71.1	507	34.5	11.24	9.3
38	38	Westwood	33,459	4.5	53.7	67.6	1,678	37.4	14.66	10.0
39	40	Pleasant Ridge	10,181	15.9	62.9	71.7	456	30.48	17.98	12.7
40	35	College Hill	17,264	33.9	60.5	68.6	1,153	28.53	11.70	4.8
41	33.5	Mt. Airy	8,199	10.2	66.9	72.6	496	40.92	10.28	4.4

Socio-Economic Status Rank 1970	1980	Statis-tical Neigh-borhood	Popu-lation 1980	% Black	Percent High School Graduates (25 years or older) 1970	1980	Total no.	Not Enrolled in school %	Not High School Grad. %	Jobless (Unem-ployed or not Labor Force) %
42	47	Hyde Park	14,955	3.8	76.0	84.8	707	18.4	4.24	0.6
43	41	North Avondale-Paddock Hills	6,762	53.0	69.4	78.6	916	8.2	2.2	2.2
44	44	Mt. Wash-ington	11,632	0.5	66.6	74.7	600	42.2	20.16	9.2
CITY OF CINCINNATI			385,457	34.0	50.9	57.9	27,508	31.7	18.0	12.6
SMSA			1,401,491	12.0	48.4	63.3	105,595	29.7	13.1	8.6

*Asterisk indicates name change from 1970 to 1980

[1] Queensgate population is primarily institutional. This neighborhood had only five households in 1980. As of 1980, Cincinnati is considered to have 47 residential neigh-borhoods, not including Queensgate. In 1980, the number was 44.

[2] Roselawn's 1980 SES rank excludes consideration of data for tract 62.02 (Longview Hospital). 1970 rank includes 62.02.

SOURCE: Census of population and housing (PHC80-2-121), 1980, U.S. Department of Commerce , Bureau of the Census . 1970 SES Rank: The Social Areas of Cincinna-ti, by Michael E. Maloney, Cincinnati Human Relations Commission, 1974. 1980 SES Rank: The Social Areas of Cincinnati, 1980, forthcoming publication by the same author. Data for Cincinnati portion of split tracts is deleted.

Although high school dropout rates tend to vary directly with the SES rank of the neighborhood, the data show that there are exceptions. For example, Mt. Washington, which had the highest SES rank of all Cincinnati neighborhoods, had a 1980 dropout rate of 20.2, higher than for the West End, which had a 1970 SES rank of 7 (44 being the highest, 1 the lowest rank) and dropout rate of 17.8.

The other exception to dropout rates varying according to SES is that dropout rates in some Appalachian neighborhoods are even higher than their SES rankings would indicate. For example, Carthage had a 1970 SES rank of 17, but its dropout rate in 1980 is 8th highest in the city at 40.1. Eight of the ten neighborhoods with dropout rates above 40% are predominantly Appalachian (see Table 11:2). Appalachian and Black are not mutually exclusive terms, of course. Over-the-Rhine, for example, has thousands of Blacks with roots in Appalachia.

Among the predominantly Black neighborhoods, North Fairmont, English Woods, and Over-the-Rhine have extremely high dropout rates (Table 11:2). However, there are some pleasant surprises that may indicate effective efforts to promote school attendance among Black youth. South Cumminsville, West End, Avondale, Evanston, Bond Hill, Kennedy Heights, and Madisonville have dropout rates of less than 20%. Winton Hills, Fay Apartments, Mount Auburn, Walnut Hills, and Corryville are in the 20-25 percent range. These rates, of course, should not be considered as acceptable.

TABLE 11:2

SES RANK (1970) AND DROPOUT RATE RANK (1980) FOR THE TEN
NEIGHBORHOODS WITH THE HIGHEST DROPOUT RATES

| | | | | | Predominant Ethnic Group of Dropouts | |
Neighborhood	Dropout Rate	Dropout Rate Rank	SES Rank	Percent Black	White Appal.	Black Appal.
Lower Price Hill	57.8	1	3	0.5	X	
Sedamsville-Riverside	50.2	2	8	0.7	X	
Camp Washington	49.6	3	1	10.5	X	
N. Fairmont-English Woods	48.4	4	4	60.9		X
South Fairmont	46.8	5	13	5.8	X	
Over-the-Rhine	44.8	6	9	66.7		X
Riverside-Saylor Park	42.9	7	15	6.2	X	
Carthage	40.1	8	17	0.0	X	
East End	36.5	9	2	12.6	X	
Northside	32.7	10	21	12.4	X	

NOTE: For both Dropout rate and SES rank, 1=worst case. Queensgate with a dropout rate of 66.2 was deleted because youth population is institutional. Camp Washington also has an institutional population (CCI) but is also a residential community with high dropout rates.

ADULT EDUCATION LEVELS. Table 11:2 shows the percentage of the adult (over 25 years of age) population in each census tract and neighborhood for 1970 and 1980. Tract numbers for 1970 and 1980 show changes in census tract designations made between the two censuses.

Both the lower and higher SES tracts and neighborhoods tended to increase their percentage of high school graduates significantly during the decade. In order to interpret the full meaning of these data, some questions need to be answered for each neighborhood. Tract 8 in the West End, for example, went from 19.4% high school graduates in 1970 to 14.7% in 1980. Did more young people fail to complete school or did the better-educated people move out of the tract? Did the tract boundary change? Is this an urban renewal area?

The two tracts in Bond Hill showed relatively little change during the decade. Is this because the neighborhood is very stable? Are younger presumably better-educated people moving out or going away to college? The tracts in Fairview-Clifton Heights had such a dramatic improvement in education levels that one should ask whether "gentrification" is taking place. Or is the improvement mostly due to younger people staying in school longer? Note that the youth dropout rate is still relatively high in Fairview-Clifton Heights (18.2%).

The summary statistics at the end of Table 11:2 show that in 1970, Cincinnati was ahead of the SMSA in percent of high school graduates. By 1980, Cincinnati had fallen behind the metropolitan area as a whole. As of 1980, only 57.9% of Cincinnatians over 25 had a high school education compared to 63.3 in the SMSA. No doubt, migration is a factor in the relative decline for central city, but, regardless of the causes, this decline has serious implications.

A comparison of dropout statistics between the two censuses is made difficult by the fact that the 1970 census lists 16-17-year-old and 16-21-year-old dropouts. From the 1980 census, we can get 16-19-year-old groups which cannot be compared to the 1970 groupings. Nonetheless, these figures are useful because they clearly indicate the nature of the neighborhood climate for school achievement.

It is fair to say that in a "typical" Cincinnati census tract only about half of the population are graduates of high school and that about one-third of the young people are dropouts by the time they are 19. Dropout rates continue to be highest in White Appalachian tracts. The highest dropout rate in 1980 (excluding Queensgate) was in tract 10 in Over-the-Rhine (64.4): tract 91 in Lower Price Hill (52.8) was second. Tract 10 is Appalachian (Black and White) and Black, and Lower Price Hill is Appalachian White.

The pattern of Appalachian dropouts shows up in the middle as well as in the lower socioeconomic range. Carthage, Avondale, Evanston, East Price Hill, and Northside are comparable socioeconomically, but the heavily White Appalachian

CIVILIANS, 16-19 YEARS OF AGE

	Not in School	Not High School Graduates
East Price Hill	745	335
Westwood	627	247
Northside	437	293
Avondale	418	281
Over-the-Rhine	415	319
West Price Hill	408	195

tracts generally have higher dropout rates than predominantly Black tracts of comparable SES.

Of the 8,702 16-19-year-olds in the city in 1980, approximately 3,854 are estimated to be Black and 4,848 Appalachian White or Other White.

In each of these six neighborhoods, the number of dropouts, even when one omits those under 16 and over 19, is large enough to justify the operation of a special high school or major adult education facility. In the Western Hills plateau area, there are nearly 2,000 out of school youth of whom 777 dropped out before completing high school. Similar area concentrations exist in such neighborhoods as Avondale, Walnut Hills, Evanston, Mt. Auburn, Corryville, and Madisonville on the east side of the city, as well as in Northside and surrounding areas.

For those interested in comparing Cincinnati dropout statistics with Central Appalachian counties, another study is of interest. The University of Kentucky Appalachian Center has published a study of dropout rates for related counties in Eastern Kentucky, Tennessee, Virginia, and West Virginia. The Central Appalachian study uses census data on 16-19-year-olds and shows, for example, a 30.7 average dropout rate for Eastern Kentucky Appalachian counties. Dropout rates in the 18 "worst case" Kentucky counties range between 35.9 (deKalb, Tennessee), and 49.9 (Clay, Kentucky). By comparison, Cincinnati's 11 "worst case" neighborhoods have 16-19-year-old dropout rates ranging from 32.7 (Northside) to 57.8 (Lower Price Hill). The Cincinnati system is hardly outperforming the poorest counties in Central Appalachia in retaining Appalachian youth through the 12th grade. Although the nature of schooling and the organization of schools may be different in urban as opposed to rural schools, the point remains: the schools must address the issue of the uneven educational attainment of their students.

IMPLICATIONS. Only about half adult Cincinnatians have a high school education, and nearly one in five of Cincinnati 16-19-year-olds are school dropouts. Whether one considers the ideal of free and universal education, looks at education as a means to produce a highly trained labor force, or views schooling as a vehicle for the prevention of social problems, the conclusion is the same. The community needs to take concrete steps to provide a higher level of education for its population.

When one adds to the statistics presented in this report the knowledge that many of our high school graduates are ill-prepared for college, jobs, or further vocational training, Cincinnati's situation could be considered one of crisis proportions. The first step in the search for solutions is to acknowledge that a problem exists.

One definition of a problem is that a problem is merely the absence of an idea. One idea that seems to be working on a small scale is the network of community-based education centers sponsored by the Urban Appalachian Council, the Episcopal Diocese of Southern Ohio, Santa Maria Community Services, Cincinnati Union Bethel, and similar programs which provide Adult Basic Education and G.E.D. preparation. These and other programs need to be expanded and their efforts more broadly supported with public and private funds. Public and private schools need to do more to keep young people in school and our colleges and universities need to do more of the kind of linking with neighborhood-based programs that Xavier and the University College at the University of Cincinnati are trying to implement in Lower Price Hill and Northside. In these programs, counseling and instruction are carried out in the neighborhood setting by university-trained personnel. Students, the majority of whom are completing a high school equivalency curriculum, are in this way prepared to take the next step – attendance at a local college or university. The Cincinnati community can take advantage of the new national interest in adult literacy by becoming an innovator in this field.

12

APPALACHIAN YOUTH IN CULTURAL TRANSITION

Clyde B. McCoy & H. Virginia McCoy

Education has received considerable attention in the literature on Appalachian youth. Much of the literature points to cultural differences which created problems for Appalachian youth in school. Language or accents of first-generation youth (and some second-generation youth, as well) set them apart immediately (Rhodes, 1968; Wagner, 1974, 1975). Misinterpretation of mountain dialect, idiomatic expressions, accent differences, and other cultural differences cause problems in relationships of Appalachian youth with urban peers and school personnel (McCoy and Watkins, 1979).

Appalachian culture places emphasis on individual achievement and the value of self-sufficiency – Appalachians are not "joiners" and do not relate readily to group activities. Appalachian youth are less likely to seek, or readily accept, school personnel support, such as sponsorship or encouragement by a particular teacher or counselor; they try to deal with problems on their own. They are less likely to participate in school activities (Rhodes, 1968; Wagner, 1975), and parents are less likely to participate in PTA's (Watkins, 1976). Youth do not identify with their schools, especially in junior and senior high school (Miller, 1979), since most youth are placed in an unfamiliar neighborhood for those grades. In addition, since few youth participate in school activities, few are in positions of leadership to serve as role models for others. Parents are overwhelmed by school bureaucracy, by unfamiliar extra-curricular activities, and by the educational jargon of such groups. Class differences in terms of a mother's employment may conflict with meeting times and may preclude a work schedule to attend those meetings.

High absenteeism and truancy are related to the cultural value placed on the importance of the family, as well as to the traditional migration process. Familism requires that family situations take priority over education (and in many cases, jobs). High absenteeism (Adams, 1971; Wagner, 1974; Rhodes, 1968) is, at least in part, a result of youth being needed at home to help care for siblings and household matters. The traditional migration process, in the three to five years after initial settlement in urban areas, involves frequent relocation (Schwarzweller, 1970). A family's adjustment to an urban area can mean moving several times to find satisfactory neighborhoods, jobs, schools, doctors, and shopping areas. "Indifference" or lack of interest in education was cited by many authors as one of the prevailing features of Appalachian youth in school (Wagner, 1974, 1975; Huelsman, 1969; Henderson, 1966; Moore, 1976). This attitude was described in various ways, as youth feeling ambivalent toward school, being shy, reticent, passive, avoiding conflict, and withdrawing. Few, however, perceived the significance of cultural conflict. Appalachian parents see more value in basic education and skills development than in extra-curricular activities and abstract idea training (Miller, 1977). Parents may encourage Appalachian students into career/practical skills and vocational classes rather than college preparatory or advanced placement classes.

Parents often sacrifice personal needs in order to have their children achieve the educational level equivalent to their own (Adams, 1971). However, the low educational level of Appalachians, traditionally, complicates parents' commitment to higher education (Miller, 1977). Kunkin and Byrne found that the parents without high school degrees considered education irrelevant (Kunkin and Byrne, 1973).

Moore and Pastoor (1976) were interested in whether educational values of Appalachian youth were retained in an urban setting. They compared sixth graders in Perry County, Kentucky, and Cincinnati, Ohio, and found that both groups felt that education was moderately important to their lives. Urban youth, however, felt more positive toward education than rural youth, in that urban youth had more confidence in their teachers' abilities and urban students were more inclined to aspire toward a college education. But based upon current evidence, urban Appalachian youth are frustrated in accomplishing such goals.

Appalachian students have also experienced difficulty in racial, class, and cultural conflicts. Wagner (1975) says, in describing the typical Appalachian student in his sample:

> If he attends a school where there are blacks, he will not understand the blacks and will tend to keep to himself or to associate only with other white students. If he is placed in a threatening situation, he will normally withdraw, not because he is afraid, but because he does not understand the more aggressive behavior of black students. If pressed too hard, he will simply take action to avoid future incidents (such as avoiding the lunchroom, the front hall, or, in the extreme situation, quit attending school.)

Appalachians have traditionally had little experience with urban blacks, since the black population in the Appalachian region is relatively small. Miller explains that this lack of experience continues in urban schools in elementary grades since Appalachian children attend school with other Appalachians in their own neighborhoods. However, contact increases at the junior high school level where white Appalachians often constitute a minority in the schools. Since the junior high and high schools take Appalachian youth out of their own neighborhood, away from their own "turf," they become fearful, believe rumors of reprisals, and generally feel intimidated.

Class differences cause Appalachian youth to feel "looked down on"and the lack of attention given to Appalachian culture only adds to a defeated self-image. Differences in language, dress, and values are seen by other classes as deficiencies or inferiority (Miller, 1977; 1979). These feelings of inferiority and fear were found in Cleveland to stem from the lack of skills and experiences in certain situations (Kunkin and Byrne, 1973).

The conditions affecting Appalachian youth in school have culminated in extreme dropout rates. Maloney (1974) found that all twelve of the census tracts in Cincinnati with dropout rates of 40 percent or higher were in Appalachian neighborhoods

Several authors suggested methods of working with Appalachian youth to improve educational levels, as well as relationships with school personnel and peers. Some of these solutions have been alluded to: teacher training (Adams, 1971; Wagner, 1974; Henderson, 1966), curriculum development (Wagner, 1974) in Appalachian culture, and the use of innovative teaching methods (Wagner, 1974). Parent and community involvement in the schools (Wagner, 1974; Henderson, 1966; Watkins, 1976) was considered important in order to provide a personal approach and commitment, as well as having parents and students feel ownership to their schools.

Future roles, expectations, and aspirations of Appalachian youth are unclear. Wagner (1975) found Appalachian youths' job aspirations to be vague and unrealistic considering low school achievement. Henderson (1966), in studying Appalachian youth, did not find any relationship between school achievement and employment aspirations. Moore and Pastoor (1976), on the other hand, observed a positive relationship between the perception of a good education and a good job among urban Appalachian youth. In addition, Ricco (1965) found a positive relationship between achievement aspirations in both Appalachian and non-Appalachian males in Whitehall, Ohio, a small urban area.

Other than school-related experiences, little information exists concerning the behavior of Appalachian youth in urban environments. However, there is some evidence that the transition from the mountains to urban life presents cultural incongruities. For example, independence and freedom of movement were allowed by parents in the Appalachian mountain environment. However, when migration occurred, the spatial restrictions of the urban setting affected this lifestyle. Parental freedom, combined with alienation experienced in the school systems, and peer pressure (Huelsman, 1969) resulted in higher delinquency rates.

Examples of cultural clashes creating adverse attitudes toward authorities among these (Appalachian) youth include domestic stress in the new environment, individualism in the face of need for legal help, and perceived prejudice in the legal system, both as to poor people and as to Appalachians in particular (McCoy, 1976).

Inner-city Appalachian youth must also deal with restricted recreational facilities. Facilities are often staffed by workers insensitive to the Appalachian value system, or are controlled by other groups.

Appalachian youth find themselves caught between the values of the urban society in which they live and the values from their heritage.

Data

This study is based on survey data collected in 1975 to assess youth behavior in four cities: Baltimore, Providence, Cincinnati, and Detroit. The National Center for Urban/Ethnic Affairs (NCUEA) developed and tested the survey instrument, and then contracted with community organizations in each city to collect the data.

NCUEA provided training and technical assistance to the community organizations during the data collection phase.

Questionnaires were administered in parochial and public schools in Detroit and Baltimore. The Providence and Cincinnati organizations were unable to obtain access to schools and utilized outreach programs to administer the questionnaire to youngsters in the community.

The out-of-school populations were selected in specific predetermined ethnic neighborhoods on the basis of a 20% sample of ethnic youths in each selected neighborhood. Interviewers were instructed to find and interview youths fourteen to twenty years old in the prescribed neighborhoods by locating youths where they were known to "hang out," such as recreation centers, bars, churches, neighborhood drop-in centers, and after-school programs.

Interviewers had to account for unique variations. For example in Cincinnati an added consideration of low educational levels among out-of-school youth meant that some interviews had to be conducted in small groups; other interviews needed to be conducted with the interviewer reading the questions and filling in the answers.

Findings

Comparisons based on the survey data and on noting similarities and differences among the various youths should provide a certain understanding of the differences in behavioral patterns between Appalachians and other urban ethnic youths and provide some further insights into the cultural transition experienced by Appalachian youths.

The sample of 1458 youths included 445 (30.5%) Appalachians, 157 (10.8%) Blacks, 307 (21.1%) Polish, and 549 (37.7%) other ethnics. Each group contained slightly more males than females: 43.4% of the Appalachians were females, 44.5% blacks, 48.8% Polish, and 45.6% other ethnics.

The median ages of the ethnic groups in the sample are shown below. Appalachian youths were the oldest in the sample, with a median age of 17.1 years. Blacks were the youngest, 16.3 years.

	Median Age
Appalachian	17.1
Black	16.3
Polish	16.6
Other	17.1
Total Sample	16.9

Religious affiliation for Appalachians and blacks was primarily Baptist, with Roman Catholicism second in importance (see Table 12:1). Polish youths were overwhelmingly Roman Catholic (90%), as were other ethnics (53.6%).

Fundamentalism underlies the religious beliefs of many Appalachians and strongly influences other values. These beliefs are founded on a literal interpretation of the Bible, an expectation of reward in the next life, and a world view in which God is omnipotent and man is fallible (Jones, 1978).

TABLE 12:1

RELIGION

	Appalachians		Blacks		Polish		Other	
	N	%	N	%	N	%	N	%
Baptist	138	31.7	74	48.7	1	0.3	42	7.6
Black Muslims	8	1.8	6	3.9	0	0.0	3	0.5
Church of God	26	6.0	9	5.9	4	1.3	20	3.6
Congregational	3	0.7	1	0.7	2	0.7	3	0.5
Eastern Rite Catholic	2	0.5	0	0.0	3	1.0	10	1.8
Episcopalian	11	2.5	0	0.0	0	0.0	11	2.0
Greek Orthodox	5	1.1	0	0.0	0	0.0	12	2.2
Holiness	7	1.6	3	2.0	1	0.3	2	0.4
Islamic	0	0.0	0	0.0	0	0.0	6	1.1
Jewish	12	2.8	0	0.0	1	0.3	11	2.0
Lutheran	16	3.7	3	2.0	4	1.3	31	5.6
Methodist	27	6.2	9	5.9	3	1.0	12	2.2
Presbyterian	10	2.3	2	1.3	2	0.7	1	0.3
Pentecostal	17	3.9	2	1.3	1	0.3	9	1.6
Roman Catholic	70	16.1	15	9.9	274	90.7	295	53.6
Other	31	7.1	9	5.9	1	0.3	18	3.3
None	53	12.2	19	12.5	6	2.0	50	9.1
Total	436		152		302		550	

Religion in the mountains (and transferred to the urban environment) was less focused on institutionalized ritual and ceremony than based on personalized beliefs in God, Christ, and the church. Specific and literal interpretations of the Bible have molded behaviors and emotions and have shaped a value system which permeates daily life routines.

Fundamentalist churches which were delineated in the questionnaire include Baptist, Church of God, Congregational, Holiness, and Pentecostal; 43.8% of the Appalachians and 58.6% of the blacks belonged to these churches.

The surprisingly large number of Appalachians (12.2%) who did not identify with any church may be indicative of the cultural transition Appalachian youths are experiencing. The transition from the more traditional Appalachian values to the more secular values and belief systems of urban youths could be due, in part, to influence from their peers or from obtaining a more "realistic view" of life based on their negative experiences in urban neighborhoods. The role of the church among inner-city urban youths probably reflects ambiguity as to its purpose and value for many of them. The storefront churches prevalent in many inner-city areas represent a lack of stability that does not provide for the type of support needed by the youths in confronting various situations which occur during cultural transition.

Even though religion and the development of religious values are important to Appalachians, church attendance is not. More than half the Appalachians in our study either never attended, or else, only attended services a few times in the past year (Table 12:2). Even in grade school years, church attendance was considerably less than for the other three groups. The importance of religion to Appalachians is in shaping a belief system, not in regular church attendance.

TABLE 12:2

ATTENDANCE AT RELIGIOUS SERVICES

	Appalachians		Blacks		Polish		Other	
	Grade School	Past Year	Grade School	Past Year	Grade School	Past Year	Grade School	Past Year
Never	19.4	35.1	11.3	15.8	2.3	8.3	14.6	29.4
Few times a year	19.6	28.7	12.0	24.3	5.0	23.4	15.7	31.1
About once a month	9.1	6.6	9.3	15.1	5.6	6.9	6.8	7.9
Few times a month	15.5	12.4	24.0	20.4	11.6	10.9	20.8	14.5
About once a week	36.4	17.2	43.3	24.3	75.5	50.5	42.0	17.1
N	439	442	150	152	302	303	547	544

As recent studies have revealed, Appalachian youths have substantial problems with the urban school systems. Educational attainment, measured by a median for highest grade completed, shows that Appalachians in the study had completed fewer school years than any other group, even though they were one of the oldest groups in the sample. Further, there were few Appalachians enrolled in high school academic programs or college classes (Table 12:3).

Median Highest Grade Completed

Appalachians	9.9
Black	10.1
Polish	10.6
Other Ethnic	10.3
Total Sample	10.2

Since Appalachian youths' experiences with the public school systems have been negative ones, some are apparently selecting other alternatives to complete their education. Table 12:3 shows that Appalachians (10.9%) as well as

TABLE 12:3

CURRENT SCHOOL PROGRAM

	Appalachians N	%	Black N	%	Polish N	%	Other Ethnics N	%
High School Academic	60	22.6	34	25.8	119	49.0	125	35.1
General	83	31.2	47	35.6	70	28.8	102	28.7
GED	20	7.5	0	0.0	2	0.8	11	3.1
Business Course	22	8.3	14	10.6	19	7.8	41	11.5
Vocational or Trade School	29	10.9	18	13.6	7	2.9	24	6.7
College	13	4.9	6	4.5	17	7.0	26	7.3
Other	39	14.7	13	9.8	9	3.7	27	7.6
Total	438	100.0	151	100.0	303	100.0	545	100.0

Blacks (13.6%) were in trade or vocational schools. An additional 7.5% of Appalachians were enrolled in GED programs, which was a substantially higher number than for the other young people.

Debunking all the stereotypes revealed in Polish jokes, the grades reported by Polish students were substantially higher than those reported by the other groups (Table 12:4). In addition, Polish students had the highest proportion enrolled in high school academic programs with many enrolled in college programs (7.0%), as well as the highest median school years completed (10.6).

Black youths were similar to Appalachians in the area of education, reporting the lowest grades of all groups, and low median grade completed scores. None of the Black youths were enrolled in GED programs, but some, like Appalachians, were apparently selecting alternatives to the public school system in that 13.6% were in trade or vocational programs.

Over one-fourth of the youths in the sample were not in school, but were of school age. Appalachians comprised 49.2% of these, 34.2% were other ethnics, 11.8% were Polish, and 4.7% were blacks. In revealing their reasons for not completing school, 49.2% said they had dropped out. The majority of Appalachians, Polish and other ethnics had dropped out of school, while Blacks evidenced a greater variety of reasons for being out of school, including almost a quarter whose education was disrupted by being in jail (Table 12:5).

TABLE 12:4

GRADES IN SCHOOL IN THE PREVIOUS YEAR

	Appalachians N	%	Black N	%	Polish N	%	Other Ethnics N	%
Fail	36	8.2	8	5.3	9	3.0	35	6.4
D Average	52	11.9	15	9.9	16	5.3	68	12.5
C Average	206	47.0	88	58.3	110	36.3	245	45.0
B Average	105	24.0	34	22.50	132	43.6	162	29.7
A Average	39	8.9	6	4.0	36	11.9	35	6.4
Total	266	100.0	132	100.0	243	100.0	356	100.0

TABLE 12:5

REASONS FOR NOT COMPLETING SCHOOL

	Appalachians N	%	Black N	%	Polish N	%	Other Ethnics N	%
Dropped Out	108	57.8	3	16.7	26	57.8	58	44.6
Suspended/ Expelled	12	6.4	3	16.7	4	8.9	29	22.3
Hospitalized	20	10.7	2	11.1	2	4.4	5	3.8
Jail	20	10.7	4	22.2	3	6.7	14	11.5
Other	27	14.4	6	33.3	10	22.2	24	18.5
Total	187		18		45		130	

The post-high school plans of respondents (Table 12:6) show realistic expectations of Appalachian youths, especially in light of their current educational experiences. Only 16.2% planned to go to college, while nearly one-fourth planned to go to work. Of the Appalachians, 20.7% had no plans after high school and 12.7% did not plan to go to complete high school–not an encouraging picture for further educational achievements. In light of Moore's (1976) finding that urban youths aspired more toward a college education than rural Appalachian youths, the youths in this study, who are older, have apparently reduced their expectations by the time they reach high school age. Low expectations, however, may also be a reflection of fatalism, another prominent value among many others discussed by Jones (1978).

More Black youths and Polish youths planned to attend college than to go to work. Their higher expectations for the future are also revealed in the small number who look forward to a future without a high school diploma.

TABLE 12:6

PLANS AFTER HIGH SCHOOL

	Appalachians		Black		Polish		Other Ethnics	
	N	%	N	%	N	%	N	%
Academic College	61	16.2	50	35.5	82	30.4	80	16.8
Vocational Training	30	8.0	10	7.1	20	7.4	41	8.6
Work	93	24.7	27	19.1	62	23.0	107	22.5
Go into Business	11	2.9	6	4.3	10	3.7	35	7.4
Marry/Raise Family	14	3.7	2	1.4	14	5.2	20	4.2
Join Army	24	6.4	9	6.4	19	7.0	33	6.9
Other	18	4.8	9	6.4	10	3.7	15	3.2
Don't Know	78	20.7	24	17.0	44	16.3	107	22.5
Don't Plan to Graduate	48	12.7	4	2.8	9	3.3	37	7.8
Total N	377		141		270		475	

Current employment data show that Polish and other ethnic youths had the highest proportions employed (Table 12:7). Appalachians, on the other hand, had the highest unemployment. Appalachians, traditionally, have tended not to seek jobs through state employment services or employment agencies, but have utilized the kin and friend network to find jobs (Schwarzweller and Brown, 1970). This method of finding jobs is not nearly as productive in times of high unemployment as when jobs are plentiful, and may be part of the explanation for the high number of unemployed Appalachian youths.

The conditions of inner-city Appalachian youths in this survey reveal some very discouraging patterns. The culture of Appalachian youths is undergoing change. This process of change in the urban environment has created new situations with which a changing culture must deal, but the Appalachian youths in this survey were armed with few resources for this task other than support from family and their own inner strength. In summary, the findings showed that Appalachian youths had completed fewer school grades than the comparative groups, although they were older in age. Few were enrolled in high school academic programs; however, some were selecting vocational education and GED programs as alternatives. More of the Appalachians than other groups were school dropouts, and many of those who were in school had either no plans or low expectations for their future. Some

EMPLOYMENT

	Appalachians		Black		Polish		Other Ethnics	
	N	%	N	%	N	%	N	%
Part-Time	78	29.0	25	50.0	88	57.1	116	38.3
Full-Time	62	23.0	6	12.0	30	19.5	93	30.7
Homemaker	18	6.7	1	2.0	4	2.6	10	3.3
Not in School/Not Employed	111	41.3	18	36.0	32	20.8	84	27.7
Total N	269	100.0	50	100.0	154	100.0	303	100.0

did plan to go to college and about one-fourth planned to work. However, if the high unemployment of this young age group is any indication of what the future holds, their chances for employment in adult life will be less than other groups.

Implications For The Future Of Appalachian Youth

The above research findings show consistently, that compared to other urban ethnic youths, Appalachians exhibit great symptomic behavior, indicating severe difficulties in coping with urban environments.

Why these greater difficulties of adjustment should exist for urban Appalachian youths is not clear at the present time. Further study is needed to understand the relationship between these behaviors, patterns, and the differences in cultural conditions for Appalachian youths. The recency of the migrant experience of Appalachians relative to other ethnic youths is certainly one factor that need to be considered. Empirical confirmation is needed to determine more specifically what accounts for these differences. Conflict with public institutions (in particular, the school system) is a critical factor in any attempt to understand Appalachian youths. Consistent evidence exists that Appalachian youngsters have high dropout rates, above average truancy rates, and in general, are dissatisfied with school.

Many Appalachians do not have the family and religious support systems that are needed to address medical, social, and psychological needs.

Only a proper understanding of Appalachian culture and the needs of Appalachian peoples will permit the development of appropriate community support systems. Several factors have been cited as significant to the design of support systems intended to serve urban communities containing large numbers of Appalachians.

These systems should be:

1. FAMILY AND KINSHIP ORIENTED
   Family and kinship networks have been an important source of support for mountain families (Brown, 1970). In making the transition from mountain lifeways, there is a deterioration of these kinship support networks. The University of Kentucky Medical Center and the Betheseda North Hospital in Cincinnati found that by developing a familial orientation of health delivery, the services and responsiveness among Appalachian families improved (Watkins, 1973).

2. COMMUNITY AND NEIGHBORHOOD BASED*
   Support systems for Appalachians should be neighborhood based, rather than being associated with the presently structured schools or other institutions. Experience has shown that Appalachians respond best to services that are located near their homes. In Cincinnati in recent years, response by Appalachians has been favorable to programs like youth drop-in services, community organizing, and cultural heritage projects whose primary functions are based upon self and family defined needs. Human services or referrals to such agencies are provided as a secondary function. Self-involvement has served to instill ownership in the programs by Appalachians, as well as helping them to feel that they have given something in return for the services received.

3. CULTURALLY SENSITIVE*
   Cultural sensitivity is another important characteristic of a support network responsive to the need of Appalachians. Cultural sensitivity does not necessarily mean that a program would be culturally specific. A program within the Appalachian community would need to deal with several variants of Appalachian culture, as well as other ethnic groups.

4. NON-BUREAUCRATIC*
   Another factor that is necessary in providing services to Appalachian youths in particular, is that support systems should be flexible, open, personal, and family oriented. A personal approach has been described by David Looff (1971) in his work with mountain children. He strongly emphasizes the Appalachian characteristics of personal support and familism as crucial to his success in working with the children. Youths tend to respond well to approaches which recognize them as people with problems, but not when labels such as "sick" or "mentally ill" or "bad" are placed on them.

5. COMPREHENSIVE
   A fifth factor to consider in developing supports for Appalachians is suggested by James S. Brown, a long-time scholar of Appalachian

migration and migrants. He suggests that Appalachians are multiple problem families; that their arrival in the cities presents many unique problems for the family which differ for each member of the family; and that these problems are cultural inasmuch as they are economic. Urban conditions affect each member of the family in such a unique way that the support systems usually offered by kinship and family are less effective in the new environment than they were in the mountains.

Multiple, sociocultural conflicts combined with a lack of initial opportunity to gain meaningful employment create multiple problems for the family. Since the Appalachian family relied very heavily upon the support system of kinship and familism in the mountains, the conflicts and stresses confronted in the urban environment also deteriorate that support system so that it is not as effective as in the mountain tradition.

* Categories similarly named in Watkins, (1975).

Conclusions

In conclusion, an increased understanding of Appalachian culture and needs, with the provision of appropriate support systems, could improve the conditions for Appalachian youth. Although economic conditions are also part of the problem, for Appalachians, all the problems cannot be solved through economic support. Neither should these be school based at the present time due to the alienation of the youth from the schools. These supports must be rooted in the communities and neighborhoods and involve the tremendous strength that family and kinship can offer to Appalachian youths.

13

BLACK APPALACHIAN MIGRANTS

The Issue Of Dual Minority Status

William W. Philliber & Phillip J. Obermiller

A greater proportion of blacks moved out of Appalachia during the great migration of the fifties and sixties than did whites, reducing the percentage of blacks in Appalachia to 7.3% of the population by 1970 (Appalachian Regional Commission, 1971). As a result of this selectivity, blacks are more common among Appalachian migrants than among those who remained in the region. An estimated one out of five Appalachians living in Hamilton County, Ohio, for example, is black. While studies were being conducted among Appalachian migrants who were white, black migrants were either excluded from the analysis or grouped with other blacks. Too few Appalachian blacks were found in any single survey to analyze as a separate category, and researchers feared combining blacks and whites together lest the importance of origin be confounded by race. Today the educational attainment of black Appalachian migrants is substantially lower than their white counterparts (Fowler, 1980).

There are reasons to believe that black Appalachians may have little in common with white migrants. First, their origins in Appalachia were different. While most white Appalachians living in Cincinnati, for example, came from Kentucky and Tennessee (McCoy and Brown, 1981), blacks moved from Alabama, Georgia, and Mississippi (Appalachian Regional Commission, 1971; Fowler, 1976). Appalachia is not a single cultural entity and migrants from different parts of the region may be as different as Appalachians and non-Appalachians. Second, within the same part of the region black Appalachians have usually lived isolated from whites (Allen, 1974; French, 1975; Cabbell, 1980). As with the rest of the nation, blacks were excluded from the mainstream in Appalachia. Having shared little in Appalachia, it seems doubtful black and white Appalachians found much in common after they migrated. Third, although migration brought many Appalachians–black and white–to low income neighborhoods of the city, they settled apart from each other (Fowler, 1981). Blacks from Appalachia moved to black neighborhoods where they identified with, and were identified as, blacks, but perhaps not as Appalachians (Zigli, 1981).

On the other hand, there are reasons to believe that Appalachia has had an influence on black migrants similar to that of whites. One of the first studies on black culture in Appalachia concluded that while blacks were isolated, they nonetheless developed value systems similar to whites in the area (French, 1975). While the importance of such a value system has recently been a subject of criticism (Billings, 1974; Philliber, 1981) any influence it has upon the life chances of white migrants should also then be true of blacks. The only research which has analyzed black Appalachians as a separate category supports that conclusion. Fowler's (1981) study of residential distribution found that both black and white Appalachians were more likely than their non-Appalachian counterparts to live in low-income areas of the city.

Whether blacks from Appalachia integrated into the local black community where they migrated or remained distinct because of their Appalachian heritage in the same manner as white migrants remains an unanswered question. The purpose of this paper is to provide a partial answer to that question by analyzing the socioeconomic attainments of black Appalachian migrants in Hamilton County, Ohio, relative to non-Appalachian blacks, white Appalachians, and non-Appalachian whites.

Data

Data were obtained by combining three surveys conducted in Hamilton County, Ohio. They were the 1971 Model Cities Survey (Sherrill, 1972), the 1975 Cincinnati Area Project (Philliber, 1981), and the 1980 Greater Cincinnati Survey (Obermiller, 1982). While neither methods of sampling nor measurement were the same, combining the studies produced 113 black Appalachians. That yielded a large enough group to provide a basis for at least some tentative observations.

There are four differences in the ways the three surveys were carried out which may contribute to errors in the findings here. Two of those differences are minor and two are of some consequence. First, the Greater Cincinnati Survey was conducted by telephone, while the other two were collected in-person. Findings from telephone surveys are generally consistent with in-person interviews, so this difference should matter little (Tuchfarber and Klecka, 1976). Second, participants in the Model Cities Survey were selected as part of a multistage probability sample stratified by race; the Cincinnati Area Project used a multi-stage probability sample of blocks with quotas proportional to the population; and the Greater Cincinnati Survey selected people using Random Digit Dialing. These differences also probably matter little (Tuchfarber and Klecka, 1976; Sudman, 1966). On the other hand, the Model Cities Survey is drawn from the population living within the inner-city low-income area designated as the target for the Model Cities program while the other two studies are drawn from the population of Hamilton County. As a result, the combination of the three samples disproportionately represents people in low-income neighborhoods. Finally, the Cincinnati Area Project and the Greater Cincinnati Survey classified people as

Appalachian if they were born in Appalachia or had at least one parent born there, while the Model Cities Survey classified people as Appalachians if they had moved to Cincinnati directly from Appalachia. As a result, the Model Cities Survey classified some persons as non-Appalachians who would otherwise be Appalachian. We have no reason to believe that any of these factors seriously altered the findings, but they should be remembered before reaching any final conclusions.

Findings

Although migrants from Appalachia generally are better educated than non-migrants who remained (Larkin, 1973), Appalachians average fewer years of education than natives and other migrants in their places of destination (Philliber, 1981). Table 13:1 shows that only 58% of the white Appalachians in the three studies had completed high school, but 78% of other whites graduated. However, while white Appalachians are left at a competitive disadvantage to other whites, black Appalachians are not much different from other blacks. 38% of the black Appalachians compared to 39% of other blacks were high school graduates. Both groups are seriously less educated than whites, but their differences from each other are small.

TABLE 13:1

PERCENT HIGH SCHOOL GRADUATES BY RACE AND APPALACHIAN HERITAGE

Race	Appalachian	Other
Black	35% (101)	39% (380)
White	58% (359)	78% (1,015)

TABLE 13:2

PERCENT OF LABOR FORCE EMPLOYED IN SKILLED TRADES OR WHITE COLLAR POSITIONS BY RACE AND APPALACHIAN HERITAGE

Race	Appalachian	Other
Black	41% (54)	30% (231)
White	60% (248)	81% (783)

The same pattern emerges with respect to occupational attainment among those in the labor force. White Appalachians have a lower percentage employed as white-collar workers or in skilled trades than non-Appalachian whites have, 60% and 81%, respectively. Both black groups have even fewer such employees. All but 41% of the black Appalachians and 30% of other blacks are employed in semi-skilled or unskilled jobs. Although the difference between the two black groups is still small, it should be noted that what difference does exist is in favor of black Appalachians.

The pattern is repeated in family incomes. The average annual income of other whites in the three surveys was $16,470. White Appalachians had average annual incomes of $14,182. Both black groups were considerably poorer. The average family income of black Appalachians was $7,742 and the income of other blacks averaged $6,719.

TABLE 13:3

AVERAGE INCOME BY RACE AND APPALACHIAN HERITAGE

Race	Appalachian	Other
Black	$ 7,742 (98)	$ 6,719 (403)
White	$14,182 (366)	16,470 (1,017)

TABLE 13:4

RELATIVE ATTAINMENTS OF BLACK APPALACHIANS, WHITE APPALACHIANS, & OTHER BLACKS AS A PERCENTAGE OF THE ATTAINMENTS OF OTHER WHITES

Group	Education	Job	Income
Black Appalachian	45%	51%	47%
Other Black	50%	37%	41%
White Appalachian	74%	74%	86%
Other White	100%	100%	100%

Table 13:4 summarized relative attainments of the four groups. On each of the three variables non-Appalachian whites averaged higher achievements than other groups. 78% were high school graduates, 81% had white-collar or skilled jobs, and the group averaged $16,470 in family income. If these figures are set equal to 100%, then the relative attainments of white Appalachians are shown to be about three-quarters of

the attainments of other whites. Each of the surveys used in this study have previously been analyzed to show the relative attainments of white Appalachians so these findings are not new. They are reported here only to provide a ready comparison with black Appalachians.

The data collected from black Appalachians are not entirely consistent. Black Appalachians have fewer high school graduates, but better jobs and higher incomes than do other blacks. However, none of the differences within the black group are actually very large. When the attainments of either group are compared to non-Appalachian whites, both groups are shown to have half or less of what non-Appalachian whites have. Their differences from each other are trivial when compared to their differences from whites.

It should be noted that the higher socioeconomic attainments of non-Appalachian whites can not be explained by age or by length of residence. In each of the three studies no significant differences existed for either of these variables. The explanation for the advantage of non-Appalachian whites lies in other directions.

Conclusion

The best conclusion from this study of the relative attainments of black Appalachians is that black Appalachians experience the same life chances as other blacks. They are restricted by being black, but they are not further restricted because they are Appalachian. The ethnogenesis which is characteristic of working class and poor white Appalachians is not shared by Appalachians who are blacks. Black Appalachians have become a part of the larger black group.

There are two factors which may explain why black Appalachians are not distinct from other blacks in the same way Appalachian and non-Appalachian whites are. First, ethnogenesis is partially the result of labeling and discrimination by others. White Appalachians were singled out from the general white population by stereotyping and discrimination, thereby giving impetus to the formation of a group identity (c.f. Chapter Three). Black Appalachians were not similarly distinguished from the general black population; labeling and discrimination affected all members of that group equally; giving no momentum to the rise of a separate black Appalachian identity.

But ethnogenesis can also come from stereotyping and discrimination which is internal to the group itself (Obermiller, 1982). In this case, race recedes in importance and socioeconomic stratification becomes critical. Intergroup labeling among white Appalachians in urban areas is quite negative and originates in the higher status cohort. The absence of large differences in socioeconomic status among blacks in the county, particularly when compared to whites residents, may lead to a diminution of intergroup stereotyping. This phenomenon may account for the absence of ethnogenesis among black Appalachians (Lewis, 1978). For both of these reasons, Appalachian blacks do not appear to have emerged as a group separate from blacks who are non-Appalachian.

CONCLUSION:

The Future For Appalachians In Urban Areas

William W. Philliber

There is probably little consensus on what the future holds, or should hold, for people of Appalachian heritage living outside the region. In most of the cities where Appalachians migrated little recognition appears to be made of the thousands of people who came from Appalachia. Fifteen years ago the popular press was filled with journalistic tales of Appalachians moving to Chicago, Detroit, Cincinnati, and other cities of the Midwest. Political organizers and social service providers directed efforts to reaching this population. Times have changed, and interest in Appalachians outside of the region is waning.

There is little to indicate that Appalachians moving from the region thought of themselves as a group. They identified with family and community, but region of origin was not important. The recognition and treatment of Appalachians in urban areas as a group came from the outside. The journalists came first. The newspapers of Cincinnati, Chicago, Detroit, and Cleveland carried stories of "hillbillies" who had moved to Uptown, Over-the-Rhine, and other inner city neighborhoods of those Midwestern cities. Appalachians were the "in-topic" and feature articles were found in all the newspapers of these cities. The service providers came next. Agency heads in the neighborhoods where Appalachians settled tried to understand this new clientele. What they seemed to have in common was an origin in the mountains of the southern part of the United States. They had little education, seemed to be hard workers, stuck together in family groups, and had little familiarity with urban ways. Programs were called for to service the needs of this new population. Both journalists and service providers looked at Appalachians and saw a social problem.

Social scientists in the sixties and seventies began to develop theoretical models to explain the behavior of Appalachians. Brown and his colleagues were especially interested in the family structure of Appalachians. The concept of the stem family was introduced. Appalachians were characterized as strong extended families with roots in

Appalachia and branches in the cities of the Midwest. A reciprocal relationship existed between these parts providing support as needed from one part to the other. In the seventies the emphasis on family declined and a new emphasis on ethnicity emerged.

The ethnic model provided some new approaches to the understanding of Appalachians in urban areas. For the first time Appalachians were recognized as a group. They were more than people with problems in common, they were a group who at some level associated with one another in churches, bars, and neighborhoods. They married other people with Appalachian heritage at a rate greater than chance. They lived close to one another. At some level they even identified with others like themselves.

The basis of ethnic group formation among people with an Appalachian heritage was the treatment they received from residents in the cities to which they migrated. The cities of the Midwest had begun an economic decline at the time Appalachians migrated there in large numbers. Blacks from the South also came to these cities. Natives of Midwestern cities faced economic threats from the declining economic base of the region. Because Blacks and Appalachians had just arrived in those cities they were recognized as the cause of the problem. Hillbillies became a target of discrimination. Negative stereotypes were used to characterize these people in the same way that recent European and Asian immigrants were characterized in other cities. These negative images created and reinforced the belief that Appalachians were unsuited for employment and probably unsuited for life in the city as well. Discrimination against them became common. The reaction to that discrimination brought Appalachians together resulting in the formation of an urban ethnic group.

The ethnic model shifted attention from Appalachians to the urban milieu. Earlier approaches had seen the problems of Appalachians resulting from their inability to adjust to urban life and the solution to their problems in the strengths of their families and character.

The ethnic model saw the experiences of Appalachians resulting from the treatment they received from other people. Their problems reflected a lack of opportunity, not a lack of ability; and the solution to those problems was in political action. The ethnic analogy provided a way of servicing the needs of Appalachian migrants and their families. In the sixties and early seventies money was directed by government and foundations to meet the needs of racial and ethnic groups. No one was interested in providing services to poor WASPs. Recognition of Appalachians as a group provided a basis for securing these funds. Organizations were founded which provided legitimate vehicles to conduct services to these people. That was yesterday.

The idealism of the sixties has been replaced with the reality of the eighties. Part of the decline in support for services to the poor is because so many programs of the sixties were fruitless. Probably the largest benefactor of those programs were the service providers who found steady work. In many cases people who were provided services would have succeeded without those services. Funding became disillusioned with the lack of success. The economic difficulties of the past decade have further eroded support for social services. High rates of inflation have reduced the real income of many families. People, insecure about their own futures, have been reluctant to press for expensive social reforms addressing issues of inequality. Finally, the civil rights movement has faced internal dissension. Instead of working together, different groups have fought between themselves over the issue of whose needs are greatest. Philosophical positions have become more important than the needs of people. The pragmatic utility of ethnicity is not what it was.

The evidence is clear that Appalachians living outside the region faced problems. The initial migrants had little education and few experiences which could provide a basis for good employment. They found work as lower blue collar laborers and housing in inner city neighborhoods. The unfortunate fact is that the children of these migrants did not fare better. They, too, left school before graduation and often faced unemployment. Subsequent generations of Appalachians continue to face such problems.

For most of the past thirty years, Appalachian migrants have been a people who didn't belong. Studies of Chicago, Cleveland, and Cincinnati clearly indicate that Appalachians were regarded as outsiders, denied access to opportunity because of their origin. At the same time they were forgotten by the region they left behind. As Appalachia became a political entity funds were funneled into the region to serve the people living in the region. Migrants were outsiders with no claim on those funds.

Two new problems emerge for descendents of Appalachians living in the cities of the Midwest. First, early migrants had a support network in the region. In the family system which Brown described relatives remained on family farms. Weekends were times to return to the mountains for social visits. Unemployment in the cities was dealt with by returning again to those same mountains where relatives would take a person in and provide food and shelter until work was once again available. Probably more important, these families provided emotional support. Life in the city wasn't expected to be pleasant and family understood the desires of mountain people forced to leave their communities.

Second- and third-generation Appalachians have lost much of this support. Close relatives who remained in the mountains have grown old and died. Parents, brothers, and sisters are city people who live in the same neighborhoods where thy live. The family farms are worked by distant cousins or have been sold to strangers. The option of returning to the region is closed. They don't belong.

The second problem occurs as each succeeding generation has less of an identification with their origin. The time is approaching when the majority of Appalachians living in urban areas are two or more generations removed from the mountains. A second-generation Appalachian's closest relative in Appalachia was a grandparent and for a third-generation migrant the closest relative was a great-grandparent. These Appalachians have grown up outside of the region. They are city people whose only contact with Appalachia comes from visits with kin. Their parents and grandparents may have identified with someplace in Appalachia but Appalachia has never been home to these people. It is a situation which has happened in every white ethnic group in America. The third generation has little identification with the region of origin from which their ancestors came.

There is another limitation which has always kept ethnicity among Appalachians at a minimum. For a century the people of Appalachia denied the existence of pluralism. In the nineteenth century when the communities around Appalachia developed strong identification with local areas in opposition to identification at a national level, Appalachians resisted. They thought of themselves as Americans. When the communities around them revolted and attempted to withdraw from the Union, Appalachians stayed. Even within the region today, Appalachians are more likely to identify themselves as Americans and less likely to identify with a region than are people in surrounding areas. This has had an effect on the development of ethnicity among Appalachians living in urban areas outside of the region. Despite the discrimination, despite the labeling, these people seldom see themselves as members of a group base on region of origin.

If the ethnic model has served its purpose and the time has come for other ways of understanding the experiences of Appalachians living outside the region, what is appropriate? This will be the issue for the next decade. Although only speculation is possible, some options already exist.

The problems of Appalachians outside the region in future years may best be understood as problems of class. Estimates differ but probably between a quarter and a half of the people with Appalachian origins remain in low income neighborhoods of Midwestern cities. One of the greatest disappointments has been the lack of upward mobility among succeeding generations of people of Appalachian origin. A major cause lies in the tendency to leave school before graduation. Manufacturing has become technologically demanding. People without education simply lack the skills to operate the machinery industry requires. The only jobs available for people without education are in service areas and unskilled labor. These jobs bring low pay and frequent layoffs. For many Appalachian people this has become their fate.

In a sense these people have melted into the inner city neighborhoods where they live. They have grown up on the streets. They are probably not identified as Appalachians by others; they have neither strange accents nor rural ways which make them stand out from other natives of the cities where they live. When they think of where they belong they are most likely to identify with the cities where they were born and raised. Appalachia is where their grandparents and maybe great-grandparents came from, but not them. They have become city people living in and identifying with the Midwest.

Many of these descendants of Appalachian migrants have become a part of the emerging urban underclass found in many of our cities. They lack the skills to succeed in a market place which has increased its technological demands. They lack identifying traits necessary for the survival of ethnicity. They have become a people society will pass by. They will continue to live in inner city neighborhoods. Trapped in a cycle of poverty, their children will suffer the same fate. They will become invisible people we will choose not to see. For these people there truly are too few tomorrows.

Cincinnati may remain an exception to this pattern. While other Midwestern cities have already assimilated their Appalachians, Appalachians in Cincinnati appear to remain a strong and viable ethnic group. There are two reasons for this difference. One of the factors in the Cincinnati experience is the existence of strong identifiable neighborhoods. The geographical layout of Cincinnati creates many residential areas easily separable from other areas. Many neighborhoods are identifiable by the type of people who live in them. Institutions like churches and neighborhood bars draw from local areas and provide a place where people come together. As a result, customs survive longer than would otherwise be expected. For example, churches provide an opportunity for singing songs learned in the mountains. Potluck dinners provide people an opportunity to socialize. What are basically rural customs survive in the churches and bars of Appalachian neighborhoods.

The second factor important in the survival of Appalachian ethnicity in Cincinnati is the presence of strong leadership. Cincinnati has people who have spent large portions of their lives in working for Appalachian people. The Urban Appalachian Council has become a well-organized and stable advocate for Appalachian issues. To a small extent, Appalachian identification has become a basis for political support. Appalachian ethnicity has not been allowed to die in Cincinnati. For these people there remain a few more tomorrows.

BIBLIOGRAPHY

Adams, James
    1971.   "Series on Appalachians in Cincinnati: children face special problems in school." Reprinted from the *Cincinnati Post and Times-Star.*

Agresta, Anthony
    1985.   "The migration turnaround: end of a phenomenon?" *Population Today,* 13:6-7.

Allen, Fayetta A.
    1974.   "Blacks in Appalachia." *The Black Scholar,* 15 (June):42-51.

Anderson, Alan B. and James S. Frieders
    1981.   *Ethnicity in Canada: Theoretical Perspectives.* Toronto: Butterworths.

Anglin, Mary.
    1983.   "Experiences of in-migrants in Appalachia." in Allen Batteau, (ed.), *Appalachia and America: Autonomy and Regional Independence.* Lexington: The University of Kentucky.

Antunes, George and Charles M. Gaitz
    1975.   "Ethnicity and participation: a study of Mexican-Americans, Blacks, and Whites." *American Journal of Sociology,* 80:1192-1211.

Appalachian Regional Commission
    1984a.   "Appalachian unemployment, November, 1983." *Appalachia,* 17:2.

    1984b.   "Projects funded in distressed counties in FY 1983." *Appalachia,* 17:6.

    1983.   "Appalachia: the economic outlook through the eighties." *Appalachia,* 17:1-14.

    1982a.   "Appalachian population and per capita money income." *Appalachia,* 16:22-23.

    1982b.   "Poverty status of household population in Appalachia." *Appalachia,* 16:24-25.

    1979a.   *Appalachia - A Reference Book.* Washington, DC: Appalachian Regional Commission.

    1979b.   *A Report to Congress on Migration.* Washington, DC: Appalachian Regional Commission.

    1971.   "Blacks in Appalachia. Population trends: 1960 to 1970." *Current Statistical Report Number 4.* Washington DC: Appalachian Regional Commission.

Appleby, Monica Kelly
    1970.   "Human development problems in Appalachia." in Max E. Glenn (ed.), *Appalachia in Transition.* St. Louis, MO: The Bethany Press.

Ball, J.C. and W.M. Bates
    1970.   "Nativity, parentage and mobility of opiate addicts." In J.C. Ball and C.D. Chambers, *The Epidemiology of Opiate Addiction in the United States, edited by J.C. Ball and C.D. Chambers* 95-111. Springfield, IL: Charles C. Thomas.

Barth, Fridrick
    1966.   *Models of Social Organization.* Glasgow: The University Press.

    1969   *Ethnic Groups and Boundaries.* Boston: Little, Brown.

Barron, Hal Seth
    1977.   "A case for Appalachian demographic history." *Appalachian Journal,* 4:208-15.

Belcher, John C.
    1962.   "Population growth and characteristics." in Thomas R. Ford (ed.), *The Southern Appalachian Region: A Survey.* Lexington: University of Kentucky Press.

Bell, Daniel
    1975.   "Ethnicity and social change." in N. Glazer and D.P. Moynihan (eds.), *Ethnicity: Theory and Experience.* Cambridge: Oxford Univeristy Press.

Berlowitz, Marvin J. and Henry Durand
    1977.   "School dropout or student punchout? A case study of the possible violation of property rights and liberties by the de facto exclusion of students from the public schools." *Working Paper #8.* Cincinnati: Urban Appalachian Council.

Beschner, George and Kerry Treasure
    (forthcoming) "Female adolescent drug use." In Friedmand, Alfred S. an Beschner, *Youth Drug Abuse: Problems, Issues and Treatment.* Edited by Alfred S. Friedman and George Beschner:4-7.

Billings, Dwight
    1974.   "Culture and poverty in Appalachia: a theoretical discussion and empirical analysis." *Social Forces,* 53:315-23.

Billings, Dwight and David Walls
    1980.   "Appalachians." in Stephan Thernstrom (ed.), *Harvard Encyclopedia of American Ethnic Groups.* Cambridge: Harvard University Press.

Billingsley, Andrew
    1968.   *Black Families in White America.* Englewood Cliffs, NJ: Prentice-Hall, Inc.

Blau, Peter and Otis Dudley Duncan
    1967.   *The American Occupational Structure.* New York: John Wiley and Sons.

Bonacich, Edna
    1972.   "A theory of ethnic antagonism: the split labor market." *American Sociological Review,* 37:547-59.

Bordwell, Ken
    1983a.   *Community Council Directory.* Department of Neighborhood Housing and Conservation, Division of Planning and Neighborhood Assistance, City of Cincinnati.

    1983b.   *Appendix to Community Council Directory.* Department of Neighborhood Housing and Conservation, Division of Planning and Community Assistance, City of Cincinnati.

Branscome, James
    1976.   "Appalachian migrants and the need for a national policy." in Bruce Ergood and Bruce E. Kuhre (eds.), *Appalachia: Social Context Past and Present,* 1st Edition. DuBuque, IA: Kendall/Hunt Publishing Company.

Breton, Raymond
    1964.   "Institutional completeness of ethnic communities and the personal relations of immigrants." *American Journal of Sociology,* 70:193-205.

Brewer, Earl D.C.
    1962.   "Religion and churches." in Thomas R. Ford (ed.), *The Southern Appalachian Region: A Survey.* Lexington: University of Kentucky Press.

Brown, James S.
    1968.   "The family behind the migrant." *Mountain Life and Work,* September 1968:4-7.

    1971.   "Population and migration changes in Appalachia." in *Changes in Rural Appalachia.* John D. Photiadis and Harry K. Schwarzweller (eds.).Philadelphia: University of Pennsylvania Press.

    1972.   "A look at the 1970 census." in David S. Walls and John B. Stephenson (eds.), *Appalachia in the Sixties: A Decade of Reawakening.* Lexington: University of Kentucky Press.

Brown, James S. and George A. Hillery
    1962.   "The Great Migration 1940-1960." in Thomas R. Ford (ed.), *The Southern Appalachian Region: A Survey.* Lexington: University of Kentucky Press.

Brown, James S. and Harry Schwarzweller
    1974.   "The Appalachian family." in Frank S. Riddel (ed.), *Appalachia: Its People, Heritage, and Problems.* DuBuque, IA: Kendall/Hunt Publishing Company.

Campbell, John C.
    1921.   *The Southern Highlander and His Homeland.* New York: The Russell Sage Foundation.

Caudill, Harry M.
  1963.   *Night Comes to the Cumberlands.* Boston: Little, Brown and
          Company.

Cabbell, Edward J.
  1980.   "Black invisibility and racism in Appalachia: An Informal Survey."
          Appalchian Journal, 8 (Autumn):48-54.

Chein, Isidor, Donald L. Gerard, Robert S. Lee and Eva Rosenfeld
  1964.   *The Road to H: Narcotics, Delinquency and Social Policy.* New York:
          Basic Books.

Chitwood, Dale D., Duane C. McBride and Clyde B. McCoy
  1976.   "The extent of substance abuse among high school students." *Miami-Dade
          Metro County School System.*

Cincinnati Human Relations Committee
  1956.   *Report of a Workshop on the Southern Mountaineer in Cincinnati.*
          Cincinnati: Cincinnati Human Relations Committee.

Cisin, I.H. and D.I. Mannheimer
  1971.   "Marijuana use among adults in a large city and suburb." *Annals of the
          New York Academy of Science* 191:222-34.

City Planning Commission
  1980.   *1980 Statistical Neighborhood Approximations.* Cincinnati: City
          Planning Commission.

Cohen, Abner
  1969.   *Custom and Politics in Urban Africa.* Berkeley: University of California
          Press.

Cohen, Stephen M. and Robert E. Kapsis
  1978.   "Participation of Blacks, Puerto Ricans, and Whites in voluntary
          associations: a test of current theories." *Social Forces* 56:1053-71.

Community Chest and Council of the Cincinnati Area
  1983.   *Regional Overview Report II: Profiles of Change, Greater Cincinnati
          Region.* Cincinnati: Community Chest and Council.

Cumberland, John H.
  1973.   *Regional Development: Experiences and Prospects in the United States of
          America.* Second Edition. The Hague: Mouton.

Darroch, A. Gordon and Wilfred B. Marston
  1971.   "The social class basis of ethnic residential segregation: the Canadian
          Case." *American Journal of Sociology,* 77:491-510.

Dasgupta, Statdal (ed.)
  1975.   *Structure and Change in Atlantic Canada.* Charlottetown: University of
          Prince Edward Island.

Davies, C.S. and Gary L. Fowler

1972.   "The disadvantaged urban migrant in Indianapolis." *Economic Geography*, 48:153-67.

Ehrlich, Howard J. and James W. Rinehart
1965.   "A brief report on the methodology of stereotype research." *Social Forces*, 43:564-75.

Eidheim, Harald
1968.   "The Lappish movement: an innovative political process." in M.J. Swartz (ed.), *Local Level Politics*. Chicago: Aldine.

Ergood, Bruce, and Bruce E. Kuhre (eds.)
1983.   *Appalachia: Social Context, Past and Present*, 2nd Edition. Dubuque, IA: Kendall/Hunt Publishing Co.

Erickson, K.T.
1976.   *Everything in its Path*. New York: Simon and Schuster.

Fisher, Stephen L.
1983.   "Victim-blaming in Appalachia: cultural theories and the southern mountaineer." in Bruce Ergood and Bruce E. Kuhre, (eds.), *Appalachia: Social Context Past and Present*. DuBuque, IA: Kendall/Hunt Publishing Co.

Flacks, Richard
1979.   "Growing up confused." in Peter I. Rose, (ed.), *Socialization and the Life Cycle*. New York: St. Martins Press.

Ford, Thomas R. (ed.)
1962.   *The Southern Appalachian Region: A Survey*. Lexington: University of Kentucky Press.

Ford, Thomas R. and Gordon F. DeJong
1963.   "The decline of fertility in the Southern Appalachian Mountain region." *Social Forces*, 42:89-96.

Fowler, Gary L.
1976.   "Regional mobility among people in Central Cincinnati." *Urban Appalachian Council Research Bulletin* (May):1-3.

1980.   *Appalachian Migration: A Review and Assessment of the Research*. Washington: Appalachian Regional Commission.

1981.   "The residential distribution of urban Appalachians." in William W. Philliber and Clyde B. McCoy (eds.), *The Invisible Minority: Urban Appalachians*. Lexington: The University Press of Kentucky.

Fowler, Gary L. and Christopher S. Davies
1972.   "The urban settlement patterns of disadvantaged migrants." *Journal of Geography*.

Francis, E.K.
1976.   *Interethnic Relations*. New York: Elsevier.

Frazier, E. Franklin
    1957.   *Black Bourgeoisie.* New York: Free Press.

French, Laurence
    1975.   "The isolated Appalachian Black community." Paper presented at the
            Annual Meeting of the Rural Sociological Society. San Francisco.

Gamson, William A.
    1968.   *Power and Discontent.* Homewood: Dorsey.

Garkovich, Lorraine
    1982.   "Kinship and return migration in eastern Kentucky." *Appalachian Journal,*
            10:62-70.

Gaventa, John.
    1980.   *Power and Powerlessness: Quiescence and Rebellion in an Appalachian
            Valley.* Urbana: University of Illinois Press.

Gazaway, Rena
    1974.   *The Longest Mile.* Baltimore: Penguin Books, Inc.

George, M.V.
    1970.   *International Migration in Canada: Demographic Analyses.* Ottawa:
            Dominion Bureau of Statistics.

Gibson, Arrell M.
    1975.   "Myth and reality of the melting pot thesis." in Emmett M. Essin, III
            (ed.), *Appalachia: Family Traditions in Transition.* Johnson City,
            TN: The East Tennessee State University Research Advisory
            Council.

Giffin, Roscoe
    1962.   "Appalachian newcomers in Cincinnati." in Thomas R. Ford (ed.), *The
            Southern Appalachian Region: A Survey.* Lexington: The
            University of Kentucky Press.

Gitlin, Todd and Nanci Hollander
    1970.   *Uptown: Poor Whites in Chicago.* New York: Harper & Row Publishers.

Glazer, Nathan and Daniel P. Moynihan
    1970.   *Beyond the Melting Pot.* Cambridge: MIT Press.

    1975.   "Introduction." in N. Glazer and D.P. Moynihan (eds.), *Ethnicity:
            Theory and Experience.* Cambridge: Oxford University Press.

Gleason, George
    1956.   *Horizons for Older People.* New York: MacMillan Publishing Company,
            Inc.

Goering, John M.
    1971.   "The emergence of ethnic interests: a case of serendipity." *Social Forces,*
            49:379-84.

Goode, William J.
    1963.   *World Revolution and Family Patterns*. New York: The Free Press.

Goodrich, Carter, Bushrod W. Allin, C. Warner Thornwaite, et al.
    1936.   Migration and Economic Opportunity: *The Report of the Study of Population Redistribution*. Philadelphia: University of Pennsylvania Press.

Gordon, Milton M.
    1964.   *Assimilation In American Life*. New York: Oxford University Press.

Guichard, Charles P. and Margaret A. Connolly
    1977.   "Ethnic group stereotypes: a new look at an old problem." *The Journal of Negro Education*, 43:344-57.

Handlin, Oscar
    1951.   *The Uprooted*. Boston: Little, Brown.

Harmeling, Mary B.
    1969.   "Social and cultural links in urban occupational adjustment of Southern Appalachian migrants." Unpublished Ph.D. dissertation, Forelhorn University.

Hechter, Michael
    1974.   "The political economy of ethnic change." *American Journal of Sociology*, 79:1151-78.

Henderson, George
    1966.   "Poor urban whites: a neglected urban problem." *Journal of Secondary Education*. 41:111-14.

Henson, Michael
    1976.   "There's nothing better to do." *Mountain Life and Work*, August:20-29.

Hershberg, Theodore, et al.
    1979.   "A tale of three cities: blacks and immigrants in Philadelphia: 1850 to 1880, 1930 and 1970." *The Annals*, 441:55-81.

Hill, David B. and Norman Luttbeg
    1980.   *Trends in American Electoral Behavior*. Itasca, IL: Peacock.

Holdrich, Martin K.
    1984.   "Trends: prospects of metropolitan growth." *American Demographics*. 6:33-37.

Horwood, Harold
    1979.   "The biggest outport." *Globe and Mail Weekend Magazine*, 29(March 31):12ff.

Huelsman, Ben R.
    1969.   "Southern mountaineers in city juvenile courts." *Federal Probation* 33:49-54.

Hyland, Gerard A.
    1970.   "Social interaction and urban opportunity: the Appalachian in-migrant in the Cincinnati central city." *Antipode,* 2:66-83.

    1972.   "A social interaction analysis of the Appalachian in-migrant." Unpublished masters thesis, University of Cincinnati, Cincinnati, Ohio.

Institute of Governmental Research.
    1978.   *A Citywide Analysis of the Service Area Monitoring Survey.* Institute of Governmental Research, University of Cincinnati.

Jones, Loyal
    1978.   "Appalachian values." *In Perspectives on Urban Appalachians,* edited by Steve Weiland and Phillip Obermiller. Cincinnati: Ohio Urban Appalachian Awareness Project.

Katz, Daniel and Kenneth Braly.
    1933.   "Racial stereotypes of one hundred college students." *Journal of Abnormal and Social Psychology,* 28:280-90.

Killian, Lewis M.
    1970.   *White Southerners.* New York: Random House.

Kilson, Martin
    1983.   "The Black bourgeoisie revisited." *Dissent,* 30:85-96.

Kleinman, P.H. and Irving Likoff
    1978.   "Ethnic differences in factors related to drug use." *Journal of Health and Social Behavior.* 19:190-199.

Knoke, David and Richard B. Felson
    1974.   "Ethnic stratification and political cleavage in the United States, 1952-1968." *American Journal of Sociology,* 80:630-42.

Kutner, Nancy G.
    1973.   "Use of an updated adjective check-list in research on ethnic stereotypes." *Social Science Quarterly,* 54:640-46.

Kunkin, Dorothy and Michael Byrne
    1973.   *Appalachians in Cleveland.* Institute for Urban Studies, the Cleveland State University.

Larkin, Robert Paul
    1973.   *Out-Migration from Altoona, Pennsylvania: Mobility Response to Changing Opportunities.* Unpublished Ph.D. Dissertation. Pennsylvania State University.

Leslie, Gerald R.
    1969.   *The Family in Social Context.* New York: Oxford University Press.

    1973.   *The Family in Social Context,* 2nd Edition. New York: Oxford University Press.

Levitt, Kari
    1960.   *Population Movements in the Atlantic Provinces*. New Brunswick:
           Atlantic Provinces Economic Council.

Lewis, Michael
    1978.   *The Culture of Inequality*. New York: Meridian Books.

    1981.   "Appalachian migration to Midwestern cities." In William W. Philliber
           and Clyde B. McCoy (eds.) *The Invisible Minority*, pp. 35-78.
           Lexington: The University Press of Kentucky.

Loof, David H.
    1971.   *Appalachian Children: The Challenge of Mental Health*. Lexington:
           University of Kentucky Press.

Longino, Charles F., Jr.
    1984.   "Migration winners and losers." *American Demographics*, 6:27-45.

Luckoff, Irving F.
    1972.   *Social and Ethnic Patterns of Reported Drug Use and Contiguity with Drug
           Users*. Washington, DC: U.S. Department of Justice, Law
           Enforcement Assistance Administration.

Lyman, Stanford M. and W.A. Douglass
    1973.   Ethnicity: strategies of collective and individual impression
           management." *Social Research*, 40:344-65.

McBride, Duane C.
    1977.   *Social Control and Drug Use*.   Ph.D. Dissertation, University of
           Kentucky.

McCoy, Candace
    1976.   "Attitudes of Appalachian youth towards legal authority." *Focus on
           Law*. 2:11-12.

McCoy, Clyde B. and James S. Brown
    1981.   "Appalachian migration to midwestern cities." In William W. Philliber
           and Clyde B. McCoy (eds.), *The Invisible Minority: Urban
           Appalachians*. Lexington: The University Press of Kentucky.

McCoy, Clyde B. and Duane C. McBride
    1976.   "Socio-cultural theories and techniques in the explanation for social
           research on drug abuse." Miami: Center for Social Research on
           Drug Abuse

    1978.   "Drug use in metropolitan society." Final report to National Institute on
           Drug Abuse. Miami: Center for Social Research on Drug Abuse.

McCoy, Clyde B. and Virginia M. Watkins
    1975.   "The migration system pattern of Southwest Ohio and its relation to
           Southern Appalachian Migration." *Research Bulletin*. Urban
           Appalachian Council.

    1981.   "Stereotypes of Appalachian migrants." In William W. Philliber and

Clyde B. McCoy (eds.), *The Invisible Minority: Urban Appalachians*. Lexington: The University Press of Kentucky.

McDonald, D.J.
1968. "Population migration and economic development in the Atlantic provinces." *Research Paper No. 6.* New Brunswick: Atlantic Provinces Economic Council.

McKay, J. and F. Lewins
1978. "Ethnicity and the ethnic group: a conceptual analysis and reformulation." *Ethnic and Racial Studies,* 1:412-27.

McKee, Dan M. and Phillip J. Obermiller
1978. 'The invisible neighborhood: Appalachians in Ohio's cities." *Research Bulletin.* Cincinnati: Urban Appalachian Council.

McKee Dan M. and Ian Robertson
1975. *Social Problems.* New York: Random House, Inc.

Maloney, Michael E.
1974. *The Social Areas of Cincinnati: Toward an Analysis of Social Needs.* Cincinnati: The Cincinnati Human Relations Commission.

1978. "The implications of Appalachian culture for social welfare practice." *Perspectives on Urban Appalachians,* edited by Steve Weiland and Phil Obermiller. Cincinnati: Ohio Urban Appalachian Awareness Project.

1979. "Just looking for a home: urban Appalachians in Ohio." *St. Luke Journal,* 22:117-41.

1981. 'The prospects for urban Appalachians." In William W. Philliber and Clyde B. McCoy (eds.), *The Invisible Minority: Urban Appalachians.* Lexington: The University of Kentucky Press.

Unpublished. *By-Laws, Urban Appalachians of Cincinnati.*

Maloney, Michael E. and Ben Huelsman
1972. "Humanism, scientism, and southern mountaineers." *Peoples Appalachia,* 2:24-27.

Marger, Martin N.
1981. "Ethnicization and urban Appalachians." *Working Paper 10.* Cincinnati: Urban Appalachian Council.

Marger, Martin N. and Phillip J. Obermiller
1983. "Urban Appalachians and Canadian Maritime migrants: a comparative study of emergent ethnicity." *International Journal of Comparative Sociology,* 24:229-43.

Massey, Douglas S.
1981. "Social class and ethnic segregation: a reconsideration of methods and conclusions." *American Sociological Review* 46:641-50.

Matthews, Elmora Messer
  1966. *Neighborhood and Kin: Life in a Tennessee Ridge Community.*
          Nashville, TN: Vanderbilt University Press.

Milbrath, Lester W. and M.L. Goel
  1977. *Political Participation: How and Why Do People Get Involved in
          Politics?* Chicago: Rand McNally.

Miller, Tommie R.
  1976. "Urban Appalachians: cultural pluralism and ethnic identity in the city."
          Unpublished M.A. thesis, University of Cincinnati.

  1977. "Education and urban Appalachian youth." Youth Services Training
          Handout. Urban Appalachian Council.

  1979a. Information obtained in discussion on Appalachian youths with Virgina
          McCoy Watkins.

  1979b. Information obtained in discussion on Appohn D. Photiadis and Harry K.
          Schwarzweller (eds.). Philadelphia: University of Pennsylvania
          Press.

Moore, Detlef H. and Dirk J. Pastoor
  1976. "Appalachian values: are they transferable from a rural to urban setting?"
          The Institute for Community Development. University of
          Louisville.

Mountain Life and Work.   1976 Special issue: *Urban Appalachians. Mountain Life and
          Work,* Vol. 52 (August).

Murdock, Steven H. and Clyde B. McCoy
  1974   "A note on the decline of Appalachian fertility, 1930-1970." *Growth and
          Change,* 5:39-42.

Neely, Sharlotte
  1979. "The ethnic entrepreneur in the urban Appalachian movement." Paper
          presented at The Annual Meeting of the American Anthropological
          Association.

Obermiller, Phillip J.
  1977. "Appalachians as an urban ethnic group: romanticism, renaissance, or
          revolution?" *Appalachian Journal,* 5:145-52.

  1981. "The question of Appalachian ethnicity." In William W. Philliber and
          Clyde B. McCoy (eds.), *The Invisible Minority: Urban
          Appalachians.* Lexington: The University Press of Kentucky.

  1982. *Labeling Urban Appalachians: The Role of Stereotypes in the Formation
          of Ethnic Group Identity.* Unpublished Ph.D. Dissertation, Union
          Graduate School.

Obermiller, Phillip J. and Robert Oldendick.
  1984. "Political activity among Appalachian migrants." *Social Science
          Quarterly,* 65:1058-64.

Parsons, Talcott
  1951.   *The Social System*. Glencoe, IL: The Free Press.

  1955a.   "The American family: its relations to personality and to the social
           structure." in Talcott Parsons and Robert E. Bales (eds.), *Family,
           Socialization and Interaction Process*. Glencoe, IL: The Free Press.

  1955b.   "Conclusion: levels of culture generality and the process of
           differentiation." in Talcott Parsons and Robert E. Bales (eds.),
           Family, Socialization and Interaction Process. Glencoe, IL: The
           Free Press.

Patterson, Orlando
  1975.   Context and choice in ethnic allegiance: a theoretical framework and
           Caribbean case study." In N. Glazer and D.P. Moynihan (eds.),
           Ethnicity: Theory and Experience. Cambridge: Harvard Univerity
           Press.

Peoples Appalachian Research Collective
  1972.   "Urban migrants: industrial heartland refugees." Special Issue. *Peoples
           Appalachia*, 2.

Peterson, Gene B., Laure M. Sharp, and Thomas F. Drury
  1977.   *Southern Newcomers to Northern Cities: Work and Social Adjustment in
           Cleveland*. New York: Praeger.

Philliber, William W.
  1981.   *Appalachian Migrants in Urban America: Cultural Conflict or Ethnic
           Group Formation?* New York: Praeger.

  1983.   "Correlates of Appalachian identification among Appalachian migrants."
           In Barry M. Buxton (ed.), *The Appalachian Experience*. Boone, NC:
           Appalachian Consortium Press.

Philliber, William W. and Clyde B. McCoy (eds.)
  1981.   *The Invisible Minority*. Lexington: The University Press of Kentucky.

Philliber, William W. and Phillip J. Obermiller
  1982.   "Black Appalachian migrants: the issue of dual minority status." In Rick
           Simon (ed.), *Critical Essays in Appalachian Life and Culture:
           Proceedings of the Fifth Annual Appalachian Studies Conference*.
           Boone, NC: Appalachian Consortium Press.

Pickard, Jerome
  1981a.   "A decade of change in Appalachia." *Appalachia*, 14:1-9.

  1981b.   "Appalachia's decade of change – a decade of inmigration." *Appalachia*,
           15:24-28.

Population Reference Bureau
  1982.   "U.S. population: where we are; where we are going." Special Issue
           Population Bulletin, Vol. 37, (June).

Reeves, David
   1976.   "Black Appalachians in the city." *Mountain Life and Work,* 52
           (August):18-19.

Rhodes, Charles
   1968.   "Appalachian child in Chicago schools." *Appalachian Advance,*
           October: 6-10.

Ricco, Anthony
   1965.   "Occupational aspirations of migrant adolescents from the Appalachian
           South." *Vocational Guidance Quarterly,* Autumn:26-30.

Robley, Bryant and Cheryl Russell
   1983.   "Trends: altered states." *American Demographics,* 5:34-36.

Rogerson, Peter A. and David A. Plane
   1985.   "Monitoring migration trends." *American Demographics,* 7:27-47.

Ryan, John P.
   1975.   *Cultural Diversity and the American Experience: Political Participation
           Among Blacks, Appalachians, and Indians.* Beverly Hills: Sage.

Sarna, Johnathon D.
   1978.   "From immigrants to ethnics: toward a new theory of 'ethnicization'."
           Ethnicity, 5:370-8.

Schwarzweller, Harry K.
   1970.   "Adaptation of Appalachian migrants to the industrial work situation: a
           case study." In *Behavior in New Environments: Adaptation of
           Migrant Populations,* edited by Eugene B. Broey. Sage
           Publications.

   1981.   "Occupational patterns of Appalachian migrants." In William W.Philliber
           and Clyde B. McCoy (eds.), *The Invisible Minority: Urban
           Appalachians.* Lexington: The University Press of Kentucky.

Schwarzweller, Harry K., James S. Brown, and J.J. Mangalam
   1971.   *Mountain Families in Transition.* University Park, PA: The Pennsylvania
           State University Press.

Shapiro, Henry D.
   1977.   "Appalachia and the idea of America: The problem of the persisting
           frontier." In J.W. Williams (ed.), *An Appalachian Symposium.*
           Boone, NC: Appalachian State University Press.

   1978.   *Appalachia On Our Mind.* Chapel Hill, NC: The University of North
           Carolina Press.

Sherrill, Samuel B.
   1972.   *Cincinnati Model Neighborhood Survey: A Statement of Research
           Objectives Methodology.* Cincinnati: Institute for Metropolitan
           Studies, University of Cincinnati.

Shibutani, Tamotsu and Kian M. Kwan
   1965.   *Ethnic Stratification.* New York: MacMillan.

Simpkins, O. Norman
    1974.   "An informal, incomplete introduction to Appalachian culture." In
               Marshall University Distinguished Reading Series 2. Huntington,
               WV

Spicer, Edward H.
    1971.   "Persistent cultural systems: a comparative study of identity systems that
               can adapt to contrasting environments." *Science,* 1974:795-800.

Steeves, Allen D.
    1964.   "An analysis of internal migration with specific reference to the flow of
               people from the Atlantic provinces to Guelph, Ontario."
               Unpublished M.A. thesis, University of Toronto.

Stephenson, John B.
    1968.   *Shiloh: A Mountain Community.* Lexington: The University of
               Kentucky Press

Stone, Leroy O.
    1969.   *Migration in Canada: Some Regional Aspects.* Ottawa: Dominion
               Bureau of Statistics.

Sudman, Seymour
    1966.   "Probability Sampling with quotas." *Journal of the American Statistical
               Association,* (September):49-71.

Taylor, R.L.
    1979.   *Migration In Canada: Some Regional Aspects.* Ottawa: Dominion
               Bureau of Statistics.

Traina, Frank J.
    1980.   "The assimilation of Appalachian migrants in northern Kentucky."
               Working Paper 12. Cincinnati: Urban Appalachian Council.

Tuchfarber, Alfred and William Klecka
    1976.   *Random Digit Dialing.* Washington: Urban Institute.

Uhlenberg, Peter
    1975.   "Noneconomic determinants of nonmigration: sociological considerations
               for migration theory." *Rural Sociology,* 38:296-311.

Urban Appalachian Council
    1979.   *Urban Appalachian Council 1978 Annual Report.* Cincinnati: Urban
               Appalachian Council.

Vailliant, G.E.
    1966.   "Parent-child cultural disparity and drug addiction." *Journal of Nervous and
               Mental Diseases.* 142-534-9.

Vance, Rupert B.
    1962.   "The region: a new survey." In Thomas R. Ford (ed.), *The Southern
               Appalachian Region: A Survey.* Lexington: University of
               Kentucky Press.

van den Berghe, Pierre L.
    1978.   *Race and Racism*. New York: Wiley.

Vincent, George E.
    1898.   "A retarded frontier." *American Journal of Sociology,* 4:1-29.

Wagner, Thomas E.
    1973.   "A study of selected Appalachian migrant students attending urban junior high shools in the Cincinnati, Ohio, area." Unpublished DED. Dissertation, University of Cincinnati.

    1974.   "Report of the Appalachian school study project." *Urban Appalachian Council Working Paper No. 4.* June.

    1975.   "Urban Appalachian school children: the least understood of all." *Urban Appalachian Council Working Paper No. 6.* January.

Walls, David S.
    1977.   "On the naming of Appalachia." In J.W. Williamson (ed.), *An Appalachian Symposium*. Boone, NC: Appalachian State University Press.

Ward, David
    1971.   *Cities and Immigrants*. New York: Oxford University Press.

Watkins, Virginia McCoy
    1973.   "Consideration of factors relevant to the development of health support systems for Appalachian migrants." Master's Thesis, University of Cincinnati.

Watkins, Virginia M. and Diana G. Trevino
    1982.   "Occupational and employment status of Appalachian migrant women." In Rick Simon (ed.), *Critical Essays in Appalachian Life and Culture: Proceedings of the Fifth Annual Appalachian Studies Conference*. Boone, NC: Appalachian Consortium Press.

Watkins, Virginia McCoy and Clyde B. McCoy
    1979.   *Drug Use Among Urban Ethnic Youth*. Report to the National Institute on Drug Abuse. (January).

    1980.   *Drug Use Among Appalachian Youth*. Services Research Monograph. National Institute on Drug Abuse.

Watkins, Virginia McCoy and Ray West
    1976.   "Relationships and potentials between the urban Appalachian family and the neighborhood school and neighborhood stability." Case study prepared for the National Center for Urban Ethnic Affairs. *Urban Appalachian Council.*

Watts, Ann DeWitt
    1981.   "Cities and their place in southern Appalachia." *Appalachian Journal,* 8:105-18.

Weller, Jack
    1966.   *Yesterday's People.* Lexington: The University of Kentucky Press.

    1975.   "Urbanization and the disappearance of a heritage." In Emmett M. Essin, III (ed.), *Appalachia: Family Traditions in Transition.* Johnson City, TN: The East Tennessee State University Research Advisory Council.

Weller, Robert H. and Leon F. Bouvier
    1981.   *Population: Demography and Policy.* New York: St. Martins Press.

White, Stephen E.
    1983.   "Return migration to Appalachian Kentucky: an atypical case of nonmetropolitan migration reversal." *Rural Sociology,* 48:471-91.

Williams, J. Allen, Jr. and Louis St. Peter
    1977.   "Ethnicity and socioeconomic status as determinants of social participation: a test of the interaction hypothesis." *Social Science Quarterly,* 57:892-98.

Williams, J. Allen, Jr., Nicholas Babchuk, and David R. Johnson
    1973.   "Voluntary associations and minority status: a comparative analysis of Anglo, Black, and Mexican Americans." *American Sociological Review,* 38:637-46.

Williams, Robin
    1979.   "Structure and process in ethnic relations: increased knowledge and unanswered question." Paper presented at the Annual Meeting of the American Sociological Association.

Wirth, Louis
    1938.   "Urbanism as a way of life." *American Journal of Sociology,* 44:1-24.

Yancey, W.L., E.P. Ericksen, and R.N. Juliani
    1976.   "Emergent ethnicity: a review and reformulation." *American Sociological Review,* 41:351-403.

Yinger, J. Milton
    1976.   "Ethnicity in complex societies: structural, cultural, and characterological factors.: In Lewis A. Coser and Otto N. Lasen (eds.). *The Uses of Controversy in Sociology.* New York: The Free Press.

Zelditch, Morris, Jr.
    1955.   "Role differentiation in the nuclear family: a comparative study." In Talcott Parsons and Robert F. Bales (eds.). *Family, Socialization and Interaction Process.* Glencoe, IL: The Free Press.

Zigli, Barbara
    1981.   "Appalachian Blacks–the 'double minority" *Cincinnati Enquirer* (May 5):A-6.

Zimmerman, Carle C.
    1947.   *Family and Civilization.* New York: Harper and Brothers.

CONTRIBUTORS

Kathryn M. Borman is Associate Professor of Education in the Department of Educational Foundations at the University of Cincinnati.

James K. Crissman is Associate Professor of Sociology in the Department of Sociology at Illinois Benedictine College.

Clyde B. McCoy is Professor of Sociology and Associate Director for Cancer Control at the Papanicolaou Comprehensive Center at the University of Miami.

Michael E. Maloney is Executive Director of the Appalachian Peoples Service Organization - Urban in Cincinnati.

Martin N. Marger is Professor of Sociology in the Department of Social Sciences at Northern Kentucky University.

H. Virginia McCoy is Visiting Assistant Professor in the Department of at Florida Atlantic University.

Sharlotte K. Neely is Associate Professor of Anthropology in the Department of Social Sciences at Northern Kentucky University.

Phillip J. Obermiller is Assistant Professor of Sociology in the Department of Social Sciences at Northern Kentucky University.

Robert W. Oldendick is Assistant Director of the Institute for Policy Research at the University of Cincinnati.

William W. Philliber is Professor and Chair of the Department of Sociology at the State University of New York at New Paltz.

Maureen R. Sullivan is Executive Director of the Urban Appalachian Council in Cincinnati.

Thomas E. Wagner is Professor of Planning and Administration and Senior Vice Provost at the University of Cincinnati.

INDEX

A

Abt Associates, 13

Academy for Contemporary Problems, 13

accent, 28, 37-41, 44, 65, 99

advocacy; organizations, 5-12, as role for outsiders, 45-46, *see also* support services

age profile of Appalachians, *see* demographic characteristics

Akron, OH, 4, 15, family type study in, 83-88

Alabama; migration patterns, 55-58

alcoholism, as stereotype, 37-38, 41

Allen-Edwards feud, 82

Anschell, Kurt, 13

apathy, as stereotype, 37-38, 41

Appalachia; definition of, 53-58, dropout rates in, 97, economy, 64, inmigration, 52, 60, migration within, 54, 55, 60-62–regions of; central, 58, 59, southern, 3, 25, 26, 52, 58, 62 northern, 59, 61

Appalachian Action Council, 12

Appalachian Alliance, 11

Appalachian Committee, 6-8, 10, 13

Appalachian Community Development Association, 9-10

Appalachian Development Projects Assembly of the Commission of Religion in Appalachia, 11

Appalachian entrepreneur, 44, 45, 47

Appalachian Festival, 8-10, 44

Appalachian Fund, 6-8

Appalachian Identity Center, 7-9, 46

Appalachian Issues Network, 11

Appalachian Migrants in Urban America: Cultural Conflict or Ethnic Group Formation?, ii, 15

Appalachian movement, urban, 5-12, 45-47

Appalachia On Our Mind, 43

Appalachian People's Service Organization–Urban Office, 11

Appalachian Regional Commission, 53, *Report to Congress on Migration*, 52

Appalachian School Project Committee, 89

Appalachians; definition of, 45-46

Appalachian Studies Conference, 11

Appalachian Women's Organization, 8

Archdiocese of Cincinnati, 6

Area-to-Area Migration Flow Data, 52-54

Arizona, migration patterns, 54-60

ascription, 43

assimilation, 30

Atlanta, GA; migration patterns, 55-58,

Appalachian movement, 46

attainment, socioeconomic, 16, 20-21,
26, 36-37, 70, of blacks, 21, 36-37,
70, and community council
participation, 74-79, of Maritimers, 26-
27, of recent migrants, 51, 64

automobile industry, 28

Ayer, Perley, 5, 6

B

Baltimore, 15, 46, migration patterns, 56-
58, youth study, 102

Barth, Frederick, 43-44

Battelle Institute, 9

Berea College, 5, 6

Bethesda North Hospital (Cincinnati), 109

Birmingham, AL, 56-58

blacks; dropout rates, 90-95, involvement
in community councils, 74-79, political
influence, 30, views of Appalachians,
37-40, youths, 102, 104-107, *see also*,
attainment, socioeconomic

black Appalachians, 90-95, 111-115,
culture, 112, education, 113, income,
114, migratory patterns, 111,
occupations, 113-114, residential
patterns, 112, studies of, 15

blaming the victim, 14, 16

Bragdon, Marshall, 5-6

Brown, Katie, 8

Brown, James, 13

Bureau of the Census, 52

C

California, migration patterns, 54-57, 59,
60

Camp Washington, 9

Career Education Program (UAC), 10

Catholics, in Cincinnati, 44, involvement
in Appalachian movement, 7

Central Ohio Appalachian Council, 11

CETA, 10

Charleston, WV, migration patterns, 57,
58

Chattanooga, TN, 57, 58

Chem Dyne industrial site, 11

Chicago, studies of, 15, Appalachian
movement in, 46, migration patterns,
56, 57, 59

Cincinnati, OH; Appalachian population
of, 4, as center of urban Appalachian
movement, 5-11, migration patterns, 4,
25-27, 56-57, youth study, 100

Cincinnati Area Project, 1975, 15, 112

Cincinnati, City of; affirmative action
policy statement, 8, City Council, 11,
Human Relations Commission, 5-9, 13,
89, Mayor's Friendly Relations
Committee, 5, 6, Public Schools, 89

Cincinnati *Enquirer*, 6

Cincinnati Union Bethel, 97

Citizen's Services Survey, 1981, 73

City Folk, 11

civil rights activism, 29

class relationships, *ii*, within urban Appalachian movement, 16, *vs* ethnicity, 16, 17, 30, 31, *see also* upward mobility, middle class Appalachians

Clermont County, OH, 15

Cleveland, OH; Appalachian movement in, 11, 12, 46, migration patterns, 4, 56, 57, 59, studies of, 15, youth, 101

Client Advocate Program (UAC), 11

coalitions of neighborhood groups (Cincinnati), 74-77

coal industry, 3, 64

Coffey, Virginia, 5, 7

Coles, Robert, 13

Columbia, SC, migration patterns, 57, 58

Columbus, OH, 4, 15, 46, Appalachian movement in, 11, migration patterns, 56, 57, 59, national conference, 9, 13

Community Chest (Cincinnati), 10, 11

Community Commitment Foundation, 8

community councils, participation in, 74-79

community organizing, 9, 11, 46, 74-79

competition for jobs, 19, 21, 36, 37, with blacks, 28

Council of the Southern Mountains, 5-7, 11

culture, Appalachian, *i*, 44, 99, 100, 108, establishing, 8, 9, existence of, 21, 27, 43-44, sensitivity to, 107

D

Dallas, TX, migration patterns, 55, 56, 58, 60

Dayton, OH, Appalachian movement in, 11, 46, migration patterns, 4, 56, 57, 59, 63, studies of, 15

Deaton, Brady, 13

delinquency, 99, 100, 101

demographic characteristics of Appalachians, 26, 36, 70-71, 73-75, studies, 15

Depression, effects on migration, 25, 26

Detroit, MI; Appalachian movement, 46, migration patterns, 56, 57, 59, 63, youth study, 102

discrimination, 4, 5, 19-22, 36

downward mobility, 16

dropout rates, 64, 89-97, 101, 106

Drug Education Program (UAC), 10

Drukker, Ray, 6

E

ecological patterns, 28-32, 40

education; Appalachian attitude towards, 99-101, studies of, 15, *see also* schools

education, lack of, as stereotype, 38

educational attainment, 16, 36, 64, 70-71, 100-101, 113, of blacks, 70, of Cincinnatians, 96-97, improving, 101, by neighborhood, 90-94, in rural Appalachia, 96 elderly, studies of, 15

Emmanuel Community Center, 6,7

endogamy, 82, 83

Episcopal Diocese of Southern Ohio, 97

ethnic boundaries, 27-28, 30-32, 35, 44

ethnic entrepreneur, 44-45, 47

ethnic group, Appalachians as, *ii*, 16, 17, 22, 46, further development, 30-31, 63-66

ethnic group formation, 19, 22, 23, 63-65, conditions for, 23, 25, cultural model, 22, 23, 25, 27, ecological model, 24, 28, ethnic boundary model, 24, 27, 35, 43, political economy explanation, 17-21, political model, 24, 29-30, 69

Ethnic Groups and Boundaries, 43

ethnicity, 16, 17, 21, 24, 27, 64, "stereotyped," 31, *see also* ethnic group formation, culture

extractive industries, 25, 26

F

Faber, Stuart, 6, 7

factionalism, 45-46

family, importance of, 21, 89, 99, 100, 109, 110

family type, 44, nuclear, 81-83, extended, 81-83, in urban milieu, 83-88, of orientation and procreation, 84-86

farming, in Maritime provinces, 25-26, in southern Appalachia, 25-26

fatalism, 21, 106

fear of institutions, 21

federal recognition of urban Appalachian movement, 9

Florida, migration patterns, 54-60

Ft. Lauderdale, 56-58, 60

Foster, Frank, 67, library on Appalachian Migrants, 11

Fowler, Gary, 13

fundamentalism, 103

G

Gallahan, Sister Shirley, 6

great migration, 3, 13, 63, 64

Greater Cincinnati Foundation, 8

Greater Cincinnati Survey, 1982, 36, 112

Greater Cincinnati Study, Fall 1980, 70

Greenville, 57

Griffin, Roscoe, 5, 13

H

Hamilton Appalachian People's Service Organization, 11

Hamilton, OH, migration patterns, 4, Appalachian movement in, 11, studies of, 15, 16

Hamilton County, OH, black Appalachians in, 111-115, political activity, 69

Hatfield-McCoy feud, 82

health, studies of, 15

Heritage Room, 8, 9

homeland, *i*, 44, 65

home ownership, 78

honesty, as stereotype, 12, 37, 38, 41

housing, studies of, 15

Houston, immigration, 56-58, 60

HUB Social Services Center, 7

Huntington, WV, migration patterns, 57, 58

I

identity, Appalachian, 7, 9, 11, 15, 20-21, 24, 28, 30, 35, 45, by out-group, 15, 28, 30, *see also* stereotypes, ethnic group

Illinois, migration patterns, 54-57, 59-60

income, 20-21, 36, 52, 70-71, 112, of recent migrants, 64

independence, 21

Inner City Neighborhood Coalition, 10

Indiana, migration patterns, 54-56, 59, 60

Indianapolis, 56, 59, 63

Institute of Govenmental Research, 74

interaction, patterns of, 22

Internal Revenue Service, 52, 53

The Invisible Minority, *ii*, 14, 15

isolation, 21, 40

J

Jacksonville, 56-58

jokes, ethnic, 20, 27

Junior League of Cincinnati, 8

K

Kentucky; migration patterns, 56-58, northern, *i*, 15

Kentucky, eastern, dropout rates, 97, migration patterns, 3, 4, 58

Kentucky Mountain Club, 11

kinfolk messages, 4

Knoxville, TN, 56, 57

Ku Klux Klan, 46

L

labor unions, 16

Lappish Movement, 44, 45

LEAA Grant for Youth Service Training, 9

Lexington, KY, 15, 19, migration patterns, 55-58

Leybourne, Grace, 13

Los Angeles, inmigration, 55-57, 59

Louisville, KY, migration patterns, 56-58, 63

loyalty, as stereotype, 37, 38

M

McCoy and Watkins, 14, 20

McCoy, Clyde, 13

Main Street Bible Center, 6

Maloney, Michael, 6-10, 44-46

Marger, Martin, 17

Maritime provinces of Canada, economy, 25, 26, outmigration, 25, 26

Maritimers, culture, 27, occupations, 25, 26, political presence, 29, residential patterns, 28, self-perception, 27, stereotypes, 28

Massachusetts, inmigration, 54

Memorial Community Center, 7

Michigan, migration patterns, 54-56, 59, 60

middle class Appalachians, 20, 26, 44, 64

migrants, *i*, *ii*, 3, 4, 19-21, generation of, 63-65, recent, 63-65, SES, 20, 21, 26, 28, 37, 41, 52, 64, 90, 94, 95, *see also* ethnic group, attainment, socioeconomic

migration, rural-to-urban, *i*, 3, 4, 20, 21, 25, 26, 52, adjustment to, 6, 7, 100, 101, 108, 109, within Appalachia, 53-60, of blacks, 19, decline in, to Midwest, 59, 60, 63, and decline in education, 90, process, 3, 4, 100, push-pull factors, 3, 25, recent, 51-60, studies of, *i*, *ii*, 13, 15, 51, 52, 53, "turnaround," 52, 60

migratory streams, 4, 51, 52, in Canada, 25, 26

Miller, Tommie, 16

Miner's Benefit Program, 8

minority group, concept of, 17

Mobile, AL, 56-58

Model Cities, 7, Survey, 1971, 112

Montgomery, AL, migration patterns, 57, 58

Morgan, Larry, 13

Mountain Life and Work, 9, 13

Mountain Families in Transition, 13

Multigenerational research, 14, 15

Mynatt, Ernie, 6, 7, 9, 45

N

Nashville, TN, inmigration, 55-58

National Center for Urban/Ethnic Affairs, 102

National Conference on Urban Appalachians, 1974, 9, 13

neighborhood, 13-15, 109, -based education, 96, 97, -based support systems, 109, Cincinnati, 74, 89-90, and dropout rates, 90-94, satisfaction with, 75, *see also* Camp Washington, Over-the-Rhine, Northside, Norwood, South Fairmont, community organizing

New Brunswick, 25

Newfoundland, 25

"Newfies," 27

New Jersey, migration flows, 54, 55, 60

New York, migration patterns, 56, 57, 59

Norfolk, VA, migration patterns, 57

North Central region, migration patterns, 59, 60

North East region, migration patterns, 59, 60

North End (of Hamilton, OH), 11

Northern Kentucky University, 13

Northside (Cincinnati), 9

Norwood, OH, 10, 16, 21

Nova Scotia, 25

O

Obermiller, Phillip, 14, 16, 17

occupational status, 16, 20, 28, 36, 70, 78, 112, 113

Office of Economic Opportunity, 13

Ohio, migration patterns, 56, 57, 59

Ohio State Appalachian Commission, 12

Ohio-Kentucky-Indiana Bluegrass Association, 11

Ontario, inmigration, 28

"optimization of interest," 31

Our Common Heritage, 11

outsiders in the urban Appalachian movement, 9, 10, 11, 45

Over-the-Rhine, 6, 7, 90, 91

P

patriotism, as stereotype, 37, 38

Pennsylvania, outmigration, 56-58

Philadelphia, 57

People's Appalachia, 13

Perry County, KY, 100

Phoenix, AZ, inmigration, 56, 57, 59, 60

Pilot Cities Center, 7

Pittsburgh, PA, Appalachian movement in, 56, 57, migration patterns, 59, 61

policy, studies of, 15

Polish youths, 102, 105

political behavior of Appalachians; affiliation, 71-73, development of, 31, effect on neighborhood council involvement, 73-75, importance of ethnic origin to, 71, involvement in, 71, studies of, 70, strength of, 29, within urban Appalachian movement, 46, *see also* solidary groups

political economy theory, 19-21

"poor whites," 17, 46

Porter, Father John, 6

ports of entry, 3, 16, 29, 64

poverty stereotype, 15, 16

poverty, studies of, 15

Prince Edward Island, 25

Providence, RI, youth study, 102

Protestants in Cincinnati, 44

R

racial conflicts, 100

racism, a stereotype, 37, 38, 40, 41

recreational facilities for youth, 101, 102

Reddin, Larry, 9

religion, 26, 102, 103, as stereotype, 37, 38, studies of, 15

residential clustering, 28, 31

resourcefulness, as stereotype, 37, 38

Richmond, VA, 56, 57

Roanoke, VA, migration patterns, 55-58

S

St. Mary's Catholic Church, 6

Santa Maria Community Services, 97

schools, Appalachians in, 13, 99, 105, 106, 108

self-image, Appalachian, 8, 45, among youth, 101

self-sufficiency, 99

Shapiro, Henry, 43

Social Areas of Cincinnati Report, 9, 13

social participation, 15

socioeconomic status, *see* attainment, socioeconomic

solidarity groups, 30

Sons and Daughters of Appalachia, 7

The South Goes North, 13

southern states, inmigration, 52, 59, 60

South Fairmont (Cincinnati), 9

Spiegel, Louise, 6, 7

stereotypes of Appalachians, 28, 30, 31, 36-40, held by blacks, 36-40, held by middle-class Appalachians, 20, 40, through jokes, 20, need to eliminate, 7, 9, 14, positive, 36-40, in scholarly writing, 35, studies of, 15, 35

"Stereotypes of Appalachian Immigrants," 14

"stereotyped ethnicity," 31

suburbanization, 16

success patterns of urban Appalachians, 14

Sullivan, Maureen, 10

support systems, 4, 99, 101, 107, 108, 109

T

Tampa/St. Petersburg, FL, inmigration, 55-58, 60

Toledo, OH, 15

Tennessee, migration patterns, 56-58, dropout rates, 97

Texas, migration flows, 54-58

Toronto, 25-29

traditionalism, 16, 21

"triage" policy, 10

U

unemployment, 65, in Appalachia, 3, in Maritime Canada, 26, among youths, 107

United Appalachians of Cincinnati, 7, 9, 45

United Way (Cleveland), 12

University of Cincinnati, 13, Behavioral Sciences Laboratory, 73, summer institutes, 9, University College, 97

University of Kentucky; Appalachian Center, 97, Medical Center, 109

upward mobility, 28, 30

Urban Appalachian Council, 5, 8, 45-47, advocacy, 9, 15, 89, growth, 9, Long Range Plan, 10, objectives, 8, research, 10, 11, 13-15, 89, turmoil within, 10

V

values of Appalachians, 16, 21, 44, 100, black Appalachians, 112

violence, as stereotype, 37-38

Virginia, migration patterns, 55-58

visibility, absence of, 30-31

VISTA, 10

W

Wagner, Thomas, 13

Washington, DC, Appalachian movement in, 46, migration patterns, 58

welfare, 16

West Palm Beach, FL, 56-58

West Virginia, migration patterns, 4, 57, 58

western states, migration patterns, 59, 60

Whitehall, OH, 101

Williams, Diane, 8

Winston-Salem, NC, area, 57

women, studies of, 15

Working in Neighborhoods, 11

World War II, effect on migration, 3, 26

X

Xavier University, 97

Y

youth, 99-110, cultural transition, 99, 100, 103, job aspirations, 101, post-high school plans, 107, religion, 102-104, relationship to school, 99, 100, studies of, 15, 102